Praise for
Full Frontal PR
Building Buzz About Your Business
by Richard Laermer

"**A great PR overview, ideal for newcomers to the industry or for veterans who want to enjoy some interesting case studies**...The book would make an effective training manual to provide to your junior team members, or a powerful tool for reaching execs who might not understand or value PR as they should."
PR News

"**The best-written, most interesting, most up-to-date manual on the PR field**—with lots of useful information for both the amateur and the pro."
Al Ries
Chairman, Ries & Ries
Coauthor, *The Fall of Advertising and the Rise of PR*

"Laermer's writing is **witty, fun, edgy**...he offers simple yet 'on-point' examples to illustrate key points."
PRWeek

"*Full Frontal PR* is **an essential read for anyone seeking buzz.** With this step-by-step guide to generating word of mouth, even those without big name agencies or bottomless PR budgets will find the media world can be their oyster."
David Neeleman
CEO, JetBlue Airways

"**If Laermer isn't the best PR professional in the business, he's awfully close.**"
Bacon's *PR Media News*

"**An excellent manifesto** for people already in the business, this is also the rare example of a book that explains PR and its burgeoning power in a way that absolutely anyone can understand."

Jonah Bloom
Executive Editor, *AdAge*
Former Editor in Chief, *PRWeek*

"*Full Frontal PR* is informative, elegantly aggressive, and right on target. **If you want to generate visibility for your business, product, or project, this is the book you really need.**"

Jodee Blanco
Author, *The Complete Guide to Book Publicity*

"What a great book! **It is about time one of these priests of public relations shared the secrets of the temple—and this book is the scroll from one of the mightiest of the PR priesthoods!** Every business leader should read this before he truly needs to."

Tad Smith
President, Reed Business Information

"Richard Laermer's clients all know that he delivers magnificent results in mysterious ways. Now it turns out there's method to the Laermer madness. In *Full Frontal PR,* he lays out **a cogent, step-by-step stratagem** that belies his shoot-from-the-hipster persona."

Jon Klein
CEO, TheFeedRoom.com
Former executive producer, *CBS News*

"**This book is so good** that, given the parlous state of today's journalism, if lots of people buy it, there will be NO news on television."

Joseph DeCola
Producer, *Weekend Today*

"**Using Laermer's techniques, even an idiot like me can be hailed as an 'industry expert.'**"

Philip J. Kaplan
Founder, F———edCompany.com
Author, *F'd Companies*

"**PR is the great equalizer when competing against larger companies with deep pockets.** This book provides an engaging introduction to the fundamentals of PR and how to translate your publicity efforts into competitive advantage."

Mark Guibert
Vice President of Brand Management, RIM (BlackBerry Handheld)

"Getting serious national coverage doesn't come from who you know; it comes from what you know. *Full Frontal PR* **demystifies the task at hand by stripping the PR process of 'spin' and 'sound bites' and teaches what really matters**—creating the hook worthy of the camera and working with media to get it on air."

Jonathan Norman
Producer, *The Ellen DeGeneres Show*

"**This book has the stuff.** When E*TRADE embarked on re-launching our brand, he stepped in and provided critical strategic and creative guidance. Not only did he get us great coverage, he also ensured that we didn't miss any opportunities. This book is the real thing! Don't miss out."

Steve Abrahamson
Director of Marketing, E*TRADE Financial

"**A long-overdue primer to the most mysterious of black arts, PR, shot through with wit, wisdom, and that most rare of modern day virtues: common sense.** This should be mandatory reading for spin doctors, journalists, and, most importantly, the often hapless CEOs bounced between the rock and a very slippery place."

John Harlow
Senior Correspondent, The London *Sunday Times*

"Laermer has an unmatched knack for putting the press in the palm of your hand. He took us from obscurity to the front page of the *New York Times* in about six weeks. **Skip the B.S., slash your PR budget, and definitely buy this book.**"

Justin Kestler
Editorial Director, SparkNotes

"**Laermer shows you how to work with the media so that they'll work with you.** If you want great PR for your company, you could have someone on your payroll read this as homework"
Merrill Lynch Business Life

"For a public relations professional, Laermer might have succeeded too well with this book: **it could threaten to put firms like his own, RLM PR, out of business.**"
Publishers Weekly

"Public relations is a vastly misunderstood and underestimated art —that's right, art—that, practiced correctly, can result in enormous benefits for its practitioners and their clients. The author of *Full Frontal PR* clearly understands this concept, and he has written **an excellent guide to PR basics that demonstrates the potential power and scope of a well thought out public relations campaign.**"
Internet.com

"...Extensive media training for every executive you need to put in front of a reporter."
Ragan's Media Relations Report

"The clear layout, full of charts and checklists, explains lucidly **how to ignite and sustain a successful PR campaign.**"
MediaMap ExpertPR

"A useful and detailed plan **for anyone who wants to generate word of mouth.**"
Soundview Executive Book Summaries

"**A wizard's navigational tool kit for succeeding with media mavens, mavericks, and manipulators—elegantly.**"
Peter Guber
Chairman, Mandalay Entertainment

Full Frontal PR:
Building Buzz
About Your Business,
Your Product, or You

A complete list of our titles is available at
www.bloomberg.com/books

Full Frontal PR:
Building Buzz About Your Business, Your Product, or You

by Richard Laermer

BLOOMBERG PRESS

PRINCETON

This publication contains the author's opinion and is designed to provide accurate and authoritative information. It is sold with the understanding that the author, publisher, and Bloomberg L.P. are not engaged in rendering legal, accounting, investment-planning, or other professional advice. The reader should seek the services of a qualified professional for such advice; the author, publisher, and Bloomberg L.P. cannot be held responsible for any loss incurred as a result of specific investments or planning decisions made by the reader.

First edition published 2003, First paperback edition published 2004

1 3 5 7 9 10 8 6 4 2

Library of Congress Cataloging-in-Publication Data

Laermer, Richard
     Full frontal PR : building buzz about your business, your product, or you / Richard Laermer. -- 1st paperback ed.
          p. cm.
Includes bibliographical references and index.
     ISBN 1-57660-181-1 (alk. paper)
     1. Public relations. I. Title

HD59.L32 2004
659.2--dc22   2004018340

Acquired by Kathleen A. Peterson
Edited by Rhona Ferling
Book design by Barbara Diez Goldenberg

People are always saying a paperless office is on its way.
The authors beg to differ. To emphasize our point,
we dedicate this book to Johannes Gutenberg.

He started it all.

I have to start with Mike Prichinello, who helped with nearly every chapter and left me in awe of his many powers as a marketing guru. I thank the staff and managers at RLM Public Relations and particularly Scott J. Milne, Joe Edelson, Georgette Pascale, and Erin Mitchell. The occasional "we" in this book refers to the teamwork RLM has done as a unit.

I bow my head in gratitude to John Crutcher, Kathleen Peterson, Andrew Feldman, Priscilla Treadwell, Gail Whiteside, and the other amazing folks at Bloomberg Press—Tracy Tait, Lisa Goetz, Christina Psathas—for coping with me without constant sighs, and I send a hearty "hi" to unflappable editor Rhona Ferling.

"Hey ya!" to my mate, Steve, for being himself. Yes, always, all the time.

Something that's on my mind: In the year and a half this book has been on virtual and other shelves, I've found that people have lots of ideas about how PR works and why. So "Full Frontal PR" is now a sort of verb. "Full Frontal" is not reacting but creating. When you are "Full Frontal" you aren't waiting for news to happen, you *are* the news.

"Full Frontal PR" is reinventing what you have in order to make it relevant to a newsy, cultural, or consumer need that is out there at that second. This is the path by which people begin to understand what's behind the curtain of image.

Korea, Mexico, China, Russia, India, Albania, and other countries have brought out their own *Full Frontal PR* editions (thanks Priscilla). Uncanny! America has exported many items of importance during the past 100 years—musicals, John Travolta, bad political advice, and Elmo. To be a part of international culture means more to me than I thought.

Yeah, PR shouldn't be an *American* value!

In closing I say, "Wow cool," to people who took the time to write me to say, "I get it now!"—and to groups who sat un-fidgeting while I talked up my mission here. I wrote the thing because I had a niggling thought that the question "what is PR?" had never been answered, not really. I think now it has. Agree?

Write me at richard@fullfrontalpr.com and/or subscribe to our fancy, honest, and easy-to-digest newsletter at editor@ RLMPR.com. It's free. The best thing in life.

Introduction

AH, BUZZ.

Buzz makes the world go round. Buzz sets and alters popular trends, from the cover of *New York* magazine to the conversation at cocktail parties in Malibu. But buzz is, as well, central to discussions in front of Ma's General Store about the best places for beer and nachos in Big Fork, Montana (it's Sabo's), or what really caused a slide in sales for that beleaguered Fortune 500 firm, whose profits—or lack thereof—affect millions of folks. Indeed, this thing called buzz is critical to the success of any commercial enterprise.

And that's why we're here.

So what is it ... this seemingly nebulous concept that we call

Why We Love PR...

...Simply, because of all it can do for you!

1 *Get people nationwide clamoring for your wares, turning your local father 'n' son shop into a national, never neglected, constantly referenced, known everywhere, mega brand.*

2 *Make you famous for whatever it is you do, no matter what it is.*

3 *Send your stock price through the roof. Pass the Cohibas, please.*

4 *Get your social concerns in front of your neighbors and your House representative alike.*

5 *Set the record straight.*

6 *Make a gold album shoot up the charts or get you one "win." Hollywood types call this a "break."*

7 *Incapacitate the competition and just cannibalize the bastids.*

buzz? It's something that influences much of what we think about, talk about, and read about. Why is buzz such a capitalized topic in our quixotic America? To some strange degree, it's a publicity product of our modern media-centric age, yet it is absolutely *not* superficial—or superfluous. Quite simply, you need buzz because your competitors are working day and night to generate the same. So, how do they get it—in the media and elsewhere? And how the heck can you get some?

Dreaming about buzz is easy.

Getting buzz is often a struggle for those without resources to hire a publicist or one of those fancy PR firms we always hear about. But very often the difference between success and failure for a personality, business, or product stems from what we refer to as the buzz factor: whether or not you're on the radar screen of the curious press and the adoring public. And this is the big—ahem—secret of the publicity industry: *You* can create the buzz factor yourself. Most enterprises probably do not need a large PR budget, no matter what people, well, like us, tell you. The fact is, many don't need firms to do PR for them. They can do it on their own. This book has a single goal—to show you how to create buzz and make it stick.

We believe that the current culture of mass exposure has made this something everyone wants to learn. And why not? Who doesn't want to know how to make his business a hot-ticket item with the press and customers? And how many people can actually say they have a tool that can show them how to get word of mouth rolling, quickly and inexpensively? Yet for some reason, everyone believes that creating buzz comes from some great scientific formula (ooh) and some elusive mystery (shh). Dare we say—we find that wrong.

There's no mysterious element involved in the art of creating real cool buzz. You can learn what buzz is, and, particularly important, what it is not. You will, in these pages, discover how to build relationships with reporters so you can give them the stories they want. You can use some of our proactive advice to pinpoint the true "hook" line and sink the news media into your product and service so that the messages work for your intended audience. Once you learn how to find this news hook, you can begin to put some of the other pieces into place. Simply. Before you know it, you've got buzz—created by ingenuity, and, most important, follow-through.

Then why, pray tell, is it that the best way to spread the word about your product is through the media rather than, say, through advertising? The real reason is that press coverage is implicitly more powerful. Paid-for messages are so pervasive in our media-saturated society that we often completely ignore them as they roll by. By contrast, the free press actually validates your company or product in readers' minds. It's a fact. No matter how jaded readers are, most are more inclined to believe than distrust what a journalist writes. That's why you should always aim for the legit press. It pays off in spades and is truly the most effective way to generate interest and enthusiasm for your product. Ask anybody who reads papers or watches TV: Do they believe the news or the ads?

The aim of *Full Frontal PR* is to show you how to take the hype pervading our existence and turn it to your advantage. Taking the exposure you receive and turning it into a powerful tool is the point of a successful media relations campaign. Plainly and simply, this book will teach you to do that—step by really eager step. The publicity process via the media—television, radio, newspapers, magazines, newsletters, and the Internet—is crucial for any business today. It's important to be prepared quickly to tell your story. In our approach, the emphasis is on "media relations," because, as you will soon see, it's a practically free way to *earn* media, rather than paying for it through ad campaigns or marketing schemes. Good media-generated exposure can be its own advertising or marketing campaign!

To create buzz effectively and keep it going, you also must know how to work with the media. It's crucial to understand how to speak with the press so that you (or your top people) can answer press queries on any level. Journalists, ever under the pressure of a deadline or the watchful eye of a suspicious editor, are looking for good stories ... always. They need you as much as you need them. The basic truth is that first you need to get their attention. We'll take you through all the steps involved in doing that—how to find the right reporter to write about your company, develop a news hook, "sell" your story to her, follow up post-interview, and ensure that you continue to have a successful working *relationship*—key word—with that reporter and many others.

Once you begin to get out there, you'll learn how to create exposure instantly in different markets—for example, by taking a small mention in a local paper and using it to "source file" yourself nationwide. What's source filing? A crucial term in this book, it means positioning yourself or your spokesperson as an entertaining, interesting expert, someone reporters like to have in their (electronic and otherwise) Rolodexes, to call upon for comments on future stories. Ultimately, that means more press for you and your company, and it's a great relationship-making tool.

Then there's technology, which is all over *Full Frontal PR*. The Internet has become its own exposure-generating tool, and everyone is free to take advantage of its power and reach. It can be used effectively for marketing and advertising, sure, but Web content is also the genesis of lots of exposure in its own right. As a place for exposure to start, this still-new medium is increasingly on a par with what news junkies call "the dead-tree media." Look at Matt ("President Clinton Has a Mistress") Drudge, who was once an unknown quantity in the buttoned-down world of big media and Washington politics. With his muckraking website, aided by his uncanny ability to get scoops on Beltway scandals before the big boys, he stirred the world of pundits and of national politics into a frenzy by unabashedly breaking stories before anyone else. Now Drudge is a media (old and new) player, rubbing shoulders with those who only a few years ago may have dismissed him as a hack.

In this age of the worldly Web, you can get yourself noticed by allowing key websites and magazines access to your story. Many sites package exposure on the Web as content, and millions of people flock to these key sites every day. Plus, chat rooms, bulletin board services, and other non-"brick and mortar" techniques can be used quite easily to generate quick-hit exposure. The traditional media invariably notice the latest must-know topic on the Web, and suddenly there you are, on every PC *and* on every page.

But keep in mind that the best exposure still comes from good old-fashioned word of mouth. It is a fact that the best way to generate serious buzz is to get—and keep—people talking. No matter what the project, word of mouth can take on a snowballing life of its own and make the impact of other press and marketing efforts seem comparatively small. The surprise success of movies like *The Blair Witch Project* (an 8 mm hangout in the woods?) and *Sixth Sense* (die-hard Bruce Willis?) are amazing examples of this phenomenon, and we talk about this as soon as you turn to Chapter 1. Word of mouth is crucial, and it's stunning in its potential.

Unfortunately, exposure/buzz/PR/word of mouth is not always positive. Happily, it is not static, and bad exposure or yucky press needn't control you or drive you out of business (or crazy). Learning crisis communication is important, too, and this book tells you the best way to address those situations. We also tell you how—and show you why—sometimes it's important to go with the flow.

Let's get serious. In the past year or so, corporate responsibility has become the hot issue. (Why suddenly it has, and not before, is anyone's guess.) Corporations have, in some cases, experienced serious trouble, and one of the reasons is they have not been very open with the public and the media. You often hear bigwigs at companies talk about so-called good PR, and in our estimation, spontaneity is the key to good PR. Discussing the facts and figures instead of hiding from them—showing candor instead of evasiveness—will mean reporters then want to know you. Contrary to popular belief, facts and figures can work in your favor.

The negative publicity that has happened in the besieged world of business is surely not a failure of PR but a real failure of corporate ethics. These days you see all sorts of stories that say how PR folks are keeping their clients "off the page," and yet we always believe that the best foot is one pushed forward. Forward—meaning on the mark. After all, the whole point of dealing with the media is being able to say something *before* it actually happens—not hiding behind "no comment" and waiting for the chips to fall.

In *Full Frontal PR* we speak forthrightly about a revival of the "front page rule"—meaning, if you can't bear to see your actions reported on the front page of the dailies, then you should rethink what it is you're doing. We are fairly sure our moms taught us that concept when we were kids. The simple rule of thumb following the fiascos of WorldCom, Enron, and the like is: If your internal communications differ from what you tell investors and the press, disaster is looming!

The right—often ethical or courageous—thing is to be on the lookout for potential PR disasters and avert them. Be proactive about faulty tires, questionable accounting, bad customer service that leads to customer fallout, and yeah... cease the practice, change the product, make sweeping changes, and darn it—go public with the facts before disaster strikes. Disastrous moments typically take place when you hide from a hungry media. In the business of media this thing called honesty is our friend. Say it three times.

Nothing happens by chance, *especially* exposure—don't believe it for a second. Big buzz has its risks, but mostly it delivers rewards, and it's important to understand that once you generate it you have to control the beast with fierce determination.

So once you've got the buzz going, how do you sustain it? Sustaining buzz means constantly massaging and updating your image with fresh publicity in the general press. We'll explain that, too, but in the end, you must be the one always thinking about your message: Does it work? Is it consistent? Do journalists *get* it?

In this book you will read scores of examples we've culled from our own experiences and those of our peers we really dig. We present these in order to show you how to use your—and your company's—best ideas to get the press you want and deserve, and how you can work with the media to get crucial exposure now. Our approach is practice driven. In fact, the theories are only here to make sense of the examples! This book is meant to be inspirational and "aspiration-al." You see, media relations is hard-hitting, aggressive, and provocative. This is its reputation, and this is real. There's nothing about it, however, that you cannot learn. You know, nose and grindstone and all that. Learn through education, learn by doing—if you're serious about reaching maximum exposure.

PART I

The
Dynamics
of Exposure

CHAPTER 1

Word of Mouth

A FEW YEARS BACK, the low-budget box office battering ram *The Blair Witch Project* swept through suburbia and became the chatter around town. School buses chock-full of would-be movie crashers compared rumors they'd picked up about the movie. Was it "really" the true story? Were those kids really missing in ... the woods? And did the Blair witch really live in Hoboken?

Hmm. Water-cooler conversations about the film couldn't be quenched, so with a bantam marketing budget that could support little more than buzz, *The Blair Witch Project* used word-of-mouth PR to turn over big ticket sales and humongous box office numbers.

Blair Witch serves up the lesson that exposure is not only about media coverage; the best exposure still comes from old-fashioned word of mouth. It doesn't come about by accident, though. Starting buzz on the street level is a deliberate step that needs to be as well thought out as getting yourself on the couch of the *Today* show, only even more so! Look, here you're asking an entire community to buy in, not just a producer or two.

The most efficient way to generate exposure is to get word of mouth started skillfully and maintain it with artful diligence. You can do this by using all the techniques we'll discuss later in the book, but throughout the course of this chapter, we will identify classic methods of provoking hype, one rumor at a time. The techniques here also handily blur the lines between traditional PR and marketing. This is an important distinction, for understanding both word of mouth and other aspects of PR, so let's digress for just a moment. Rather than being separate processes, PR and marketing should work with each other to strengthen a unified message. That goes against the textbook approach, but it is definitely true. Many firms we've worked with think that PR is a substitute for marketing. In some cases, management even decides not to have a sales team in place, because they think PR can drive sales right to their door. PR is *not* a direct-response medium. It builds awareness of and perception about a product in order to increase the response rate of direct-marketing campaigns. It isn't a replacement for them.

One of our clients is a serial entrepreneur who focused all his efforts on a PR launch, with nary a single marketing effort. He called us about a five-minute local TV piece that we'd arranged, which was essentially a free ad. "No one has signed up in response," he wailed. You'd think he'd know better. Bottom line: PR isn't a Band-Aid or super crazy glue for business. It must be integrated with your marketing campaigns. If you do it well, and in conjunction with marketing know-how, would-be consumers should hear your message loud and clear.

Going Verbal

NOW, LET'S GET BACK to word of mouth. One great way to start people talking is by stirring up the lexicon. Coining a great new phrase is one of the first things you should do, because putting the word out is just that. Get some influential or hip people to start using your great new word or phrase, and you'll start some powerful word-of-mouth buzz.

Being able to turn a name into a verb and convincing people to accept your trademark as the embodiment of the field you toil in isn't easy. But if you do it right, your name will be the first one that leaps to mind when consumers think of great new electronics gadgets, say, or the best store in a five-state area for stocking hard-to-find wines and beers. Then it's a short leap to associating you and your product with the industry standard.

In 1999 our firm, RLM, launched a now legendary national firm called Kozmo.com. Able to deliver any movie and Jujubes candy to go along with it (in addition to shaving cream, milk, the morning paper, and even, uh-huh, Crazy Glue) to your door in less than one hour, Kozmo.com was poised to make a fundamental change in urban living. But first people had to hear about it. We started speaking about one-hour delivery as being "Kozmo'ed." Why go to the corner store for the *Times* when you can get it Kozmo'ed? That was the idea.

The big concept we had—to start introducing the word into the vocabulary of trendy people everywhere. Hip people all over New York City began using the verb—no matter where you went, people stopped saying, "I want a delivery" and said instead, "Let's get this Kozmoed." Talk about awe-inspiring word of mouth. The term really picked up when Kozmo announced a partnership with Amazon.com. Amazon CEO Jeff Bezos saw the value in kozmo-ing his books and chainsaws, and Amazon soon reported an upswing in sales and Web traffic.

More recently, Google.com, the Internet search engine, discovered that it had become part of the Internet generation's slick new vocabulary. Hipsters in the single scene found a new use for Google's search-engine capabilities. They started using Google to pull up their dates' digital histories to find out where their mysterious strangers had been and what they'd done on some other enchanted evening. Witty culture writers at *New York* magazine, the *Los Angeles Times,* and the *Observer* picked up the "Googling" practice in the singles scene and put it into overdrive, making Google the most popular search site on the Web for a while.

When you're trying to drive buzz about your product in this way, you have to use the new word whenever you can, in conversation and in writing, to get people truly to start using it and to make it stick in the collective memory. This is not an overnight effort, but the effects can be powerful, and they can last a lifetime. For example, take the example of Marilyn Loden, author of *Implementing Diversity,* who wrote on women and diversity. She coined the phrase the "glass ceiling" to describe the barrier women had to face in the workplace, especially those who were gunning for top positions. Because it was such a vivid image of the current corporate culture, it became part of the collective conscience of the country.

But it couldn't end there. Loden knew that without support, the phrase would sputter into oblivion, and it was too important a sentiment for that. To give it life and momentum, Loden, now considered an expert in women's issues, used the term everywhere she could. It peppered her interviews and other public appearances. The media picked up on it and began to use it in the context of every woman in every business story, on the air or in the papers. Loden's work paid off, and "glass ceiling" became a two-word term everyone knows to describe a complex social issue.

Hitch Your Wagon to a Star

IF CHANGING THE LANGUAGE is one proven approach to attract attention, another is to speak your customer's language. In 2000, *BusinessWeek* inked the term "buzz marketing" across the cover of one of its April issues. The magazine was rolling the curtain back on a new technique that smart companies were using to get the style-conscious excited about their product. The idea is to get the admired or influential to talk up your brand, to make it cool and desirable.

Vespa, a kitschy European scooter company, did this with great flair. The company sent out beautiful, lanky models in droves for a drive (on scooters) through the scene-setting streets of Los Angeles. But beauties on bikes weren't enough to make an impression. To notch up the style quotient, the models would pull up to outdoor cafés in small groups, park out front, and sit down for a cup of latte and conversation about the scooters that got them there.

Eavesdroppers and gawkers in earshot of the chai-sipping Vespa models not only sucked up the vision but their conversation, too. Instantly they saw the European scooters in the same beautiful light as they saw its drivers. Vespa knows the power of influence and those who wield it, and in this case, influence lay not with the media, but with the people whom the media follows. Vespa knew how to pick a hot location, too. For a fraction of the cost of one TV ad, they had people in the most trend-setting neighborhoods clamoring for their scooters. Be on the lookout for them everywhere!

There is one important thing to remember, though: Even hypereffective word of mouth can't save a bad product. In 1995, Twentieth Century Fox was about to unwrap its latest big flick, *Nine Months,* in theaters across the country to much expected fanfare. Ironically, given the movie's parenthood subject, its salient British star, Hugh Grant, was caught canoodling—not with his superstar girlfriend, Elizabeth Hurley, but with a prostitute, just days before the launch! The "talk" swirled out of control. Papers in America and Great Britain slapped his deer-in-the-headlights look on front pages, and the rumor mill kicked into high gear.

The following week, Grant appeared on the *Tonight* show in a much-hyped appearance to talk about the allegations, his relationship with Elizabeth, his unfortunate judgment, and of course, the movie. But now here's the clincher. What Twentieth Century Fox must have chalked up as a celestial stroke of great luck turned out to have zero effect on its bottom line. Because the movie was dull and uninteresting, even the biggest gossip scandal of the year couldn't bump the numbers up.

Movie studios are often more successful than that at using word of mouth to give movies a second wind. In 2000 Warner Studios saw strangely low numbers for *Proof of Life,* starring Russell Crowe and Meg Ryan. Its box office ranking was a disappointment, given the star power of the movie. But with the advent of digital video discs, movies now have a double life after the big screen.

Before the movie went on sale in DVD format, the studio's internal press people leaked a rumor that chemistry had bubbled over between Ryan and Crowe during the shooting. The rumor created huge curiosity on the part of movie fans who wanted to see if the onscreen twinkle in their eyes seemed real, spiking sales of the flick. Or, as we heard many people say, "I had no desire to see the movie on pay-per-view or video, but then again, I *did* have to wonder … hmm." That's all you have to do: Get them to wonder.

Fan Fare

THE 2002 OSCAR AWARDS were groundbreaking, everyone said, because Denzel Washington and Halle Berry swept the Best Actor and Best Actress awards, making it the first year African-Americans took those honors together. PR pros noticed another groundbreaking occurrence, Sandra Bullock's singularly exceptional word-of-mouth campaign for Listerine's tiny new PocketPaks (or "oral care strips").

Before Sandra made it to her seat on the arm of Hugh Grant, she managed to mention her spanking-new, cool little Listerine tabs to Joan Rivers, Jules Asner, and every other camera-wielding social arbiter on the long, red carpet. The breath-mint technologists tapped into 20 million people around the world, all tuned in to see what they should be doing next to be "in." If you flipped through the channels on your remote (for those who couldn't get a ticket!), you could actually see Sandra do her shtick from channel to channel as she progressed down the red carpet.

The brilliance of it is that she didn't *obviously* plug the product. Rather, Sandra simply worked it into every conversation, offering a tab to the interviewer or marveling at its small packaging. Again, it's an example of using trendsetters to make conversation.

As a side note, we'd also like to also remind our readers that Listerine's parent company, Warner-Lambert, did a fine job of getting the little PocketPaks breath strips into the hands of dentists for nearly ten months before its release. Dentists, like our brokers, are people we supposedly trust.

But sending out samples of a product in this way is often hit-or-miss and very expensive, to boot. Warner had the money to get a mouth-enriching product into dentists' useful hands. You may not. But influencers in a town or city sure can help you get the word of mouth started.

Tying a Buzz On

OKAY, LET'S SUPPOSE you don't have access to movie stars or scooter queens. There are still plenty of ways to get the buzz going. In major cities, parties are the way to spread the word—with, of course, fancy gift baskets that are handed out at major celebratory/commemorative/charity events (the three Cs). If you know people who run those, or can get to them, and the events have some kind of tie-in to your product, give them a call and offer to help as much as you possibly can. Also, remember that influencers don't have to be on red carpets or shiny scooters. They can be anyone who sways opinion, such as your local mayor, PTA president, or smooth-talking CEO. The key is to find the person who spends the most amount of time administering to the circle you or your idea travels in.

For example, what about that longstanding and much-maligned newspaper institution: the gossip columnist? Cringe all you like, but here in New York, nothing gets the buzz on the streets flowing faster than Page Six in the *New York Post*. Everyone from Howard Stern to *Extra* recounts the missives on this page, the fertile soil where buzz takes root and grows.

But you don't have to track down a Michael Lewittes or a Richard Johnson to get serious hype, since most local papers have at least one rumor mill, if not more, for you to tap into. A note explaining what the buzz is will suffice, and if your pitch is airtight (for that you actually have to read the rest of the book), your big idea should be the talk of the town.

Gossip (see sidebar, "When You Want Someone's Attention, Just Whisper") is a powerful tool, and it rarely backfires if you wield it well. One of the first things broadcast producers do every morning is trawl the rumor columns for salacious fodder. If you've done the heavy lifting and actually managed to get your item placed with Cindy Adams, Liz Smith, or one of the other columnists out there, clip that piece fast and work it.

And put the power of time zones to work for you. When pitching a gossip piece, unless it's extremely local in subject, pitch it to a paper on the East Coast. The East Coast works three hours ahead of the rest of the country, so when your rumor hits print, you still have an hour or two to fax it to all the other news stations on the East Coast. Then you have another two hours or more to send it west, before the sun rises and Los Angeles producers broadcast their shows.

Take It to the Streets

ANOTHER GREAT WAY to create word of mouth is to take it to the streets. If you want people on the corners buzzing about your product, deliver your brand where they're standing. Guerrilla marketing, as it's called, is the practice of hitting the streets with unconventional ways of getting your brand or product noticed. It could be as simple as a sticker campaign on every lamppost and cab divider. Or, if you've got the cash, it can be more elaborate, such as Microsoft's launching Windows ME with a Sting concert. A small firm named Eisnor Interactive created one of our favorite consumer "guerrilla" hits. Eisnor introduced New York Today, a *New York Times* online service. To publicize the service, Eisnor gave out thousands of paper spoons emblazoned with www.nytoday.com on the streets of New York. When people logged on to the website they could print out a coupon for a very cheap lunch at Daily Soup, a midtown café. Spoons on the streets equaled a lot of business and a lot of talk about the site.

What if your company is somewhere between mini and Microsoft? For a midsize concept, you gotta have a gimmick. In the mid-1980s, we managed a theater company called Theater in Our Time. The concept was to cultivate new audiences for off-Broadway theatre and to charge people a little extra for a small meal and the chance afterward to meet the cast through a Q & A onstage. We chose the plays carefully—*Sex, Drugs and Rock and Roll* by one-person-showman Eric Bogosian, and the '90s classic *Miss Saigon*.

To get some real press for our little group, we invited our members for a performance of the farcical *Forbidden Broadway*, a play that hilariously lampooned the Great White Way. But we also showcased the *real* stars being lampooned. This was the first time Chita Rivera, Ann Reinking, Tony Roberts, and others had a chance to see people make fun of them, and it made people feel terrific about going to the theatre (including the lampooned stars, all of whom had a great time). Theatergoers began talking to their friends at cocktail parties about this new, offbeat theater group that had just done something fresh and unique, and the ticket sales began rising.

A successful guerrilla tactic must be memorable and have an obvious link to your brand, and it also needs to invade people's space a bit, in a respectful manner. Most people take the same path to and from work every day, stop at the same coffee

When You Want Someone's Attention, Just Whisper

Gossip columns are funny. What many consider the most trivial form of journalism is, ironically, in some ways the most powerful. Granted, syndicate doyenne Liz Smith wasn't—until last year at least—digging into the latest accounting scandal, and Cindy Adams of the New York Post *may not know when tech stocks are going to rally, but what gossip mavens in every paper do know is what the superinfluencers are up to and what trends are about to emerge from their whims. That's power!*

Gossip columns get rumor mills buzzing quicker than you can say "psst"—and a good placement with a recognized columnist can catapult you or your product into stratospheric media levels. That's how you start the ball rolling on a news item with style and verve. Say a piece of news, the juicy type, materializes for you. Suddenly you need to swing for the fences and pitch those gossip writers and columns that matter the utmost. Go get 'em, tiger! Here are the names (in no particular order) you need to know:

❑ Rush & Molloy's "Daily Dish," *New York Daily News* (syndicated)
❑ "Page Six," *New York Post,* especially Richard Johnson, Chris Wilson, Ian Spiegelman, and Paula Froelich
❑ Lorrie Lynch, *USA Weekend*

shop, and go to the same gas station, all the while listening to the same radio station. If you can shake up their routines a bit, you stand a much better chance of being *the* conversation later in the office that same day.

BigStar Entertainment, an online DVD vendor, knew that billboards and most forms of traditional advertising were passé. Passersby are immune to regular outdoor signage. When we see pop-up ads on our browsers, we immediately delete them, and we've programmed ourselves and our ReplayTV digital recorders to ignore the thirty-second advertisements during *Friends*. Big-Star decided to create a twist on the standard outdoor billboard by

- Army Archerd, *Variety*
- E! Online (www.eonline.com)
- Jeannette Walls, "The Scoop" at MSNBC and MSNBC.com
- Michael Musto, "La Dolce Musto," *The Village Voice*
- Lloyd Grove, "Lowdown," *New York Daily News*
- Marilyn Beck and Stacy Jenel Smith, "Celebrity Gossip" (syndicated)
- Suzy, *W* magazine
- Roger Friedman, Fox News, foxnews.com (Fox 411)
- Cindy Adams, *New York Post*
- Marc S. Malkin, *New York Magazine*'s Intelligencer.com
- Liz Smith and Diane Judge—the writers of the "Liz Smith" column, syndicated in seventy newspapers, including the *New York Post*
- James Barron, "Boldface Names," *The New York Times*
- Frank DiGiacomo, "The Transom," *The New York Observer*
- Media Gossip: www.medialifemagazine.com, www.iwantmedia.com, and www.poynter.org
- George Whipple, NY 1 (New York event and celebrity news)
- Elaine Dutka, "Morning Report," *Los Angeles Times*
- Gawker.com, Nick Denton's "blog" on all things New York, which covers the country and will take your suggestions and tips (nick@gawker.com)

slapping its catchy message on delivery trucks rumbling through city streets across America. The fluorescent eighteen-wheelers marked with pithy copy lit up the streets and turned heads.

The trucks created word of mouth for two reasons: The first was their wild appearance, but the second was their immense numbers, giving the perception that BigStar was the biggest thing on the Web because it was shipping truckloads of tiny DVDs everywhere and anywhere.

The truth is, those trucks were shipping everything *but* movies. BigStar worked with shipping companies to slap its moniker on every truck in a fleet, whether they were shipping lobsters or comic books. The *illusion* of thousands of BigStar DVD movies on the street created such strong buzz for the small New York company that the *Wall Street Journal* and the *New York Times* both featured the trucks on section front pages.

Billions *and Billions* of Buzz Served Here

TO TRANSLATE ALL OF THIS into buzz for your company, start off thinking big: What would it take to get your logo on the space shuttle? From there, pare your actions down to what's manageable. Maybe it's sidewalk art all over town, or midgets on roller blades handing out menus. Or a tie-in to your website: Get people on the street to tap into your site because you're offering them a huge discount to do it. Whatever.

Remember to spread the buzz to people that other people listen to, and make sure that it shakes things up and that it's completely—versus slightly—beyond what's expected. That's why, contrary to popular belief, you should *not* do limited offers. They're crass and conventional, and the best you can hope for is a great big yawn from the consumers of America. That's not the kind of mouth action you're looking for. Always search for new ways to rise above the fray, and stick with it; otherwise the next rumor or interesting thought will take away the spotlight, break up the chatter, and leave your huge idea smelling like yesterday's fad.

Yet in the end, no matter which techniques you use, and no matter what else you learn in this book, the real key to building exposure is this simple truth: Darn it, be the best at what you do. There is no substitute for quality, even with all the exposure in the world. By far, the best way to generate more attention and word of mouth is to do what you do better than anyone else and to let your customers or fans spread the word.

Today more than ever, word of mouth remains the best advertising. For instance, RLM is a relatively small company by the standards of large, worldwide, public relations corporations.

However, we get dozens of calls seeking our services every month by companies that could easily afford to go to the big guys. Sure, we promote ourselves all we can, but most of our clients come to us via other clients and sometimes even through journalists. It's an honor to have the respect of our peers and colleagues, and no amount of self-promotion would be as valuable for us as the promotion others do for us, absolutely free, based on the known quality of our work.

Quality is something people recognize, consistently, as a serious, no-BS tangible. A recent article on the differences between large and small public relations agencies bears out our point. In a recent issue of the online newsletter *ExpertPR* from MediaMap (see Chapter 9 for more on this valuable resource), Terry Frechette, a scrappy PR pro and Boston writer, mused about the issue of spending money on PR. He derived a very "'00's" theory on seeking and finding quality agencies:

> Clients know that no matter how excited a large agency seems about landing the small $5,000 a month client today, ... as soon as the economy turns around again, these smaller clients will be either dropped from the roster, or managed by the agency's interns while the executives focus on the larger, 'more important' clients. Boutique agencies always offer lower rates ... every client is important ... no matter what the economy.

In sum, he was saying: Remember that all business is about quality. That is especially true for PR, which is without a doubt the most undervalued component of marketing in any organization.

People think that PR professionals do nothing but send out releases to reporters and that editors and writers make all the news happen. Some folks feel that PR doesn't count for much, as if there were no talent or creativity involved. Hmm. Well, PR is more than just that—it encompasses dozens of avenues. Media relations, press alerts, trade shows, brand creation, marketing communications, by-line pieces, internal messaging—a PR agency must do all of these jobs superbly. Our job in the field is to fight these misconceptions of our worth and prove our value, day after day, year after year—by being pros!

And don't let people con you into believing that big always means great. Italians have an expression—*"pocchi ma buoni"*—which loosely translates to *"little but good."* We like that.

So whether you're trying to do PR yourself with a small, in-house team or you're looking to outsource, go with hungry, nimble, aggressive, and ultimately independent thinkers. That's the way to ensure your PR will be out there creating buzz for your company—ahead of your competitors and constantly in reporters' faces. Because, as anyone who's ever dabbled in PR knows, it's not that single attempt at publicity that makes your company famous. It's keeping yourself in front of the media—in their sights, on their radar screen, whatever you want to call it—all the time, every time.

Leave No Stone Unturned

THE POINT OF THIS BOOK is to leave no stone unturned in the search for PR success, the easy, not to mention thorough and successful, way. So how do you copy the things that agencies like ours do well, or that we've been successful at? First, remember that news is subjective. And in the business of promulgating news, you must always put your own spin first and listen to your gut. Don't listen to what other people say is the best story; go with your own instincts, because if this is your story, you will definitely know best.

Many times a CEO has confided an offbeat idea to us, one that his immediate reports thought was lame. We usually counsel these folks to go for the CEO's idea, unless he's an out-and-out egotist or otherwise deluded. The reason? If it's his company and his vision, he'll be passionate about it, and he may just have the idea that puts the company on the buzz map.

Show Glamorous Passion

Always be gutsy. Yes, "always" doing anything is hard to imagine, but dealing with press people is a game, and it's a two-way street that never ends. Be out there with your heart in it, don't take no or maybe for an answer, show glamorous passion, and just, well ... go for it. You'd be surprised at how many reporters or producers will stop what they're doing, sit up, and pay attention, because these people darn well respect your gumption.

Stay informed about the world (see sidebars "It Happens to Be News, Dummy" and "Cruise the News," on pages 18 and 20, respectively). We can't say this enough! Any reporter will tell you to tie your idea to a trend. Sharpen ... sharpen ... sharpen! Smart PR pros need to make trend watching a 24/7 habit. Only then will you be sharp enough to spot the fresh ideas that make your company a natural tie-in to the news.

Take the words "I don't care" out of your mouth forever. Do you hate sports? Well, before you paper your bird cage with the sports section, at least skim through it. You may find a tie-in to your company that you would never have dreamed of if you'd considered it fit only for canary carpet. By the same token, if you don't normally talk to people who are interested in arts and culture—maybe you're a techie who lives and breathes routers—start hanging out with a cultural crowd in your workplace. Or just go to a new play or art exhibit once in a while.

Everyone in the biz will tell you that reporters like to talk to well-rounded people. Plus, you'll be much more fun at parties. But if you talk nothing but gobbledygook, journalists will get bored even if their job is to cover your industry.

We also suggest identifying some well-known trend watchers whose ideas you respect and trust. Perhaps it's a pundit with political leanings similar to your own, or a writer for the *New Yorker* or *The Economist* whose work you find insightful. Or, better yet, start reading the work of writers with whom you don't

It Happens to Be News, Dummy

It's a cool world when people can talk to each other with more than just a semblance of knowledge. PR people, especially, need to be informed. That's harder to be in an info world that is, strangely, becoming overpersonalized and overcustomized. Marketers flood our mailboxes, real and virtual, with all sorts of offers customized for us alone. Hundreds, if not thousands, of websites offer services akin to My Yahoo! or mywashingtonpost. On a more profound level, the ease with which we can arrange to be spoon-fed only the information we deem worthy is a real danger, however. Suddenly you're less informed than you ought to be, or would be if you had to seek out all this information yourself. All this overcustomization has led us down a wily path of surreal and distorted knowledge.

My elders told me the folks who didn't crash and burn in the post-1929 Great Crash days were the well-informed ones: They saw the cultural indicators that told them to react—fast! In post-Crash 2000 we'd do well to follow our forefathers' advice and cull our information from broader sources.

agree, for a different perspective and a better shot at seeing the whole picture. Whomever you choose, follow their work as often as you can. Seek out their books, their articles, and their broadcast appearances. This knowledge gives you grist for all of your dealings with the media.

Here's one piece of advice that PR pros know but won't tell people outside the industry: Think kindly toward the media! Journalists aren't as jaded as you've been told or led to imagine. That "I've-heard-it-all-before" attitude doesn't exist, at least not among journalists of any repute. Faced with shrinking newsroom staffs and resources, plus far heavier workloads, journalists today can't afford that brand of cynicism. No, they want help from good sources.

Thankfully, in-the-know types are pushing for change. What's the media of the future going to be like, then? Soon interactive news will mean a broader world, allowing us to see much more than ever before. According to veteran news guys, networks will put up a "barker channel" that will steer you to interactive applications. If you want to get more information on a current event, you'd simply click on a certain spot on your screen. The result looks like Headline News, *except that you'll be able to click on the little paragraphs to get in-depth information on the story in broadcast-quality video. Dreams like that bode well for us in the news-gathering and information industry, which is exactly what PR people must match and compete with daily.*

The people who make news are coming to grips with a news flash: Digital doesn't have to mean trivial. Matt Drudge, master of all things light and airy, said a few years ago: "Sure it will be digital, but it will be larger, more gorgeous than ever before, and completely and utterly fascinating, in order to grab [the] attention of an ingrained, thrill-seeking world." And a super well-informed one at that.

One of the coolest things about being a really informed person is that you'll be brimming with fresh ideas, from fashion to corporate management. You then become one of those sources reporters love: a PR pro who tosses out interesting ideas and trends, even if they're not always linked to a story about your company or product. And voilà! You will soon become an expert in the "thought-you'd-be-interested-in-this" e-mail subject, one of our favorite things to do (except, of course, in 2001, when it became the header of an e-mail containing a huge virus). This way, the next time you call with a pitch about your company, you've already built up a reservoir of honest respect.

Cruise the News

Read the following every day, or just casually glance at each of these, and the news of that morning is yours. Staying informed is a part-time job. Don't get fired.

❑   *The Wall Street Journal* Interactive Edition
❑   MSNBC.com
❑   *The New York Times* on the Web
❑   Nikkei Net (for Asia watchers)
❑   *USA Today*
❑   *The Economist*
❑   *The Washington Post*
❑   Bloomberg.com
❑   The Street.com
❑   *BusinessWeek*
❑   Yahoo! News
❑   CBS Marketwatch
❑   BBC News
❑   CNET's News.com
❑   *Der Spiegel*
❑   CNN Fringe News
❑   *Les Echos*

Think

Make time for self-examination. Companies should view the recent rough economic times as a gift. The slower pace of activity is allowing companies to take a step back and reevaluate what they are doing and how they are doing it. This break in frenetic action is important because "with every hour in the day accounted for, we risk losing our culture and creativity," says a wonderfully profound marketing expert we know.

Being too busy for reflection happens on both a corporate and a personal level, and it has real consequences for creativity

❑ *Forbes*
❑ *El Mundo*
❑ *Financial Times*
❑ *Gazeta Mercantile*
❑ *Los Angeles Times*

And if you're a news junkie like we are, you will also want to bookmark each of these places to visit daily, and we mean even on Saturdays:

www.sjmercury.com
www.ananova.com
www.reuters.com
www.washingtonpost.com
www.sfgate.com
www.prorev.com
www.metafilter.com
www.robotwisdom.com
www.modernhumorist.com
europe.cnn.com
www.eonline.com
ea.nytimes.com/cgi-bin/poppage?position=bottom

and fresh thinking. This same smart fellow takes time each week to see his nieces and grants hours each day just to think. "Everyone I know gets on a train," he says, "and instead of contemplating something or giving their thoughts free rein, they get on their cell phones. Cell phones allow you to have conversations to pass the time, instead of passing the time in actual thought."

Speed is good in sports and fabulous in microwaves. When we begin to hurry through life, however, things get ugly. Many of the most important things in the world take time and thought! When we sacrifice that, we lose in the end, and there's nothing touchy-feely about that result. Slow down and contemplate. Your ability to create brilliant, imaginative PR—not to mention a host of other things—will only benefit.

Finally, as the sergeant said in *Hill Street Blues*, be careful out there. We mean that in the simplest manner. Don't rush into things without thinking out your message, and don't be ill prepared for even the briefest phone call. One of our folks made that dastardly error when he phoned a reporter to double-check his name, explaining helpfully, "I want to send a bylined article to you at *Forbes*." Unfortunately, the disgruntled gent on the other end of the line worked for *Fortune*.

Watch your step, watch the news, and watch your competition. We're going to show you the best ways to do all three. And once you know those basics, you can watch your sales go through the roof. And come to think of it, why stop there?

CHAPTER 2

The Press: Merchants of Exposure

IT'S NOT 2:25 A.M. The rain isn't falling sideways. There's no fedora-topped mystery man lurking in an underpass, whispering into the ear of that reporter.

That isn't how it works at all. Hollywood serves up this image of journalistic intrigue, but it's total nonsense. Everything happens by painstaking process. It's PR people like us, and ultimately you, that do the "whispering" to journalists looking for stories like yours. And trust us, they're happy to know you.

Reality Doesn't Have to Bite

TO UNDERSTAND HOW journalism works, let's talk a bit about how it doesn't work. And this way you can save a lot of money by *not* going to journalism school. First, journalists don't hide in the shadows and fraternize with some musty underground for the big scoop. They are at their desks, waiting for the phone to ring or e-mail to ping with a really good idea.

The media works like you do, hurried and under the gun, facing crazy hours and a spouse always on them to pick up milk before they come home. They also are working under sometimes trying circumstances, to the best of their abilities. Anyone who can give them a story for the day, allowing them time to breathe and to forgo the drama of late-night stints, will surely have another press clip to hang in their lobby.

When they are at a loss for news, reporters rely on creative, connected businesspeople and a gaggle of experts for the news about the topics they are most interested in. Those topics are sometimes called "beats," and often reporters will specialize in certain areas, but the stories they're after can be simply what they find interesting that day.

But getting your story above the fold (that is, the top half of the front page) doesn't happen with merely a phone call to the news desk and a snappy pitch. You have to work well with journalists, treat them properly, and deliver the goods.

At major publications and outlets—*USA Today* and *Good Morning America,* to name a couple—a single journalist's or producer's day is interrupted by hundreds of unsolicited story pitches. No other employee, except a call-center representative or a 911 operator, has to manage so many inbound calls each day. Given that scenario, face or phone time simply doesn't come easily. For journalists, looming deadlines mean the clock rules their world, too. To be successful, you have to convince them that their interaction with you isn't going to be a colossal waste of time. Instead, they have to be certain that you are going to make the second hand tick a little slower by providing exactly what they need, and by being timely and responsible. Tick. Tock.

The key is just good, old-fashioned understanding! A real pro knows that journalists have a tough job. Near-impossible deadlines, whip-cracking editors, and hundreds of less-professional pitches than yours are inbound daily to create a challenging environment that even the most fast-paced, brilliant reporter finds difficult to cope with.

This means that as your own little PR machine, the odds are stacked against you every time you pick up the phone or click *send*. But don't let any of this discourage you from pitching, because the fact is that, contrary to popular belief, journalists and publications depend on good PR sources. If you can help journalists tame the fury of their stress-filled days, they will be all ears to you.

All Ears to You

SO HOW DO YOU BEAT THE ODDS and get article after article on your product while others are getting nowhere? Simple: If it's newsworthy, people with pens and PCs will listen. So what's newsworthy to a reporter? There's no list or set of guidelines, but incorporating some of the criteria mentioned below certainly helps.

A Local Angle

Journalists have a target audience to please, so if you have news that relates specifically to what all those thousands have in common—location—you're already ahead of the game. Recently the *Jersey Journal* ran a front-page story about a 344-pound black bear found hibernating under a home. This, my friends, is definitely not national news. But for the people of Piscataway, New Jersey, a bear under a local stairway is pretty darn relevant. And if your company happens to specialize in making products that safely repel nuisance animals, you have a built-in news hook. (For more details on finding the perfect news hook, see Chapter 4, "Finding the Right News Hook.")

The Power of the Press

Why is the media the best way to spread the word about your product, rather than advertising? The simple reason is that press coverage is implicitly more powerful than advertising. Most small companies want to get noticed, and with "free media," you can do so much more than if you spent oodles of cash on an ad.

Why is media better than a full-, half-, or even quarter-page ad? Ads can cost a lot of money, of course, but they are also the part of a publication that the public most disparages. Ads are so much a part of our lives that at this point we are jaundiced and always judgmental of them. When we look at an ad, we might have a reaction, such as "that's cool" or "what?", but only rarely do we immediately run out and purchase the item.

Our love/hate relationship with the ad also makes the advertiser suspect. The subconscious reaction is, "You paid for the adver-

There's a local angle for every business story, too. In the spring of 2002, Jazzercise, the $50 million purveyor of dance aerobic classes, was brought before the San Francisco Civil Rights Commission by a local woman named Jennifer Portnick. Portnick claimed that she was denied an instructor's position with Jazzercise due to her weight and state of physical health. Jazzercise later revised its criteria for hiring instructors. (The case was never tried.) In the days after her story hit the local papers, Portnick's *own* fitness franchise saw a sizable spike in new members from the San Francisco area. Portnick benefited from her local story by signing up a wave of weighty new customers who sympathized with her plight and by damaging the competition's image in the neighborhood. Well, no one said getting coverage was always going to be pretty.

tisement only because you want us to spend money on your product." By contrast, the free press actually validates what you say about your product. No matter how cynical the reader is, he has a general predisposition to love what he reads—and best of all, to believe it's for real, if the reporter says so.

The danger, of course, is that an article may "read" like an ad, or vice versa, creating a strange, hybrid animal that is usually called an advertorial. Although they may sound appealing to you, you should avoid advertorials, because they communicate to the reader that you have paid to have someone validate you and your company. One-sided articles that say you are the "most" are poorly conceived pieces of fluff that you should avoid at all costs.

Go for the legitimate press, every time. It pays off in spades. As an important side benefit, you can save money and take some of the pressure off your overworked staff. It is truly the most effective way to generate buzz and interest in your product.

Relation to a Bigger Story

You or your product, service, pastime, or passion might not be big news on its own, but it may be "guilty" through association. Here's our favorite example. A logistics agency that helps trucks get from here to there faster ordinarily wouldn't be at all interesting from the media's point of view, but the CEO of that company might indeed be much more compelling during an emergency flood, earthquake, or tornado. That's when the evening news anchor wants to know how local and state agencies can mobilize enough food and supplies for 5,000 families affected by a sudden California earthquake.

At that moment, the CEO's and company's expertise—there all along—is suddenly hot news. The goal is to figure out how you and your company relate to what's on the front page of that day (put another way, "How topical are you?") and then to make a quick call or three before it's old news.

Celebrities

Man, people love those folks. They love to look at them, see them, blab about them, hear about their exploits and romantic pursuits .... You get it. Attaching your product to a celebrity is a time-honored tradition, and you can use it to generate your own press—for anything. Do you make hats? Well, make one for Cher, Madonna, even Sandra Bernhard, or—what the heck—Gwyneth, J.Lo, Britney, Russell, Liam, whomever. Send a few of them—gratis, of course—to some of those celebs. If you get even one of them to say something nice about your creation—to you or their representative—you have instant-gratification press! That gives you names to drop to local or national gossip columns, which are always looking for an association. Gee, you have the hottest people wearing your wares in the hottest places for all the papers to see. (Later in the book we discuss using the clips from that press coverage to get more of the same.)

One of the qualities that will distinguish you from the rest of the pack is an ability to see beyond the day's events and turn them into an angle that will perk up the ears of journalists everywhere. To do this, you need to be a voracious reader, able to skim the day's news and spot a trend in its infancy. A good PR person—you—can take the same collection of facts as someone else and rapidly see a completely different, more noteworthy event happening.

And that's not all. To turn that idea into a flesh-and-blood story, you also need a solid grasp of an individual journalist's style and content. Translation: Whether you're skimming the headlines of the *New York Times* or your local weekly rag, don't stop thinking when you finish reading the story. Try to see beyond the day's events and find a way to tie those trends to your business. You'll hook those journalists, every time.

Got Ethics?

ANOTHER BIG FALLACY about the press is that journalists have an agenda or ulterior motive when covering the news. Believe it or not, they don't want to screw you—it's that simple. Except for a handful of Beltway (Washington, D.C.) columnists, it really is true that opinion is often removed from the story. A journalist's goal is to present the most relevant facts in an easy-to-read couple of paragraphs.

The only thing a good journalist respects more than a reliable contact is that ethical code of the trade. Here is what we mean: There is *not* a fine line between truth and fantasy. It's a chasm, and writers worth their salt refuse to risk the injuries of jumping off that cliff to navigate the rocky terrain of half-truths and unproven facts. That means they want to weigh all the facts of a story and treat you fairly in the media.

This may all come as a big surprise to those of you who have suffered wrongs at the hands of the media. Plenty of businesspeople feel they've been burned by a reporter just out for a headline, and in general there's a lot of bad blood on both sides. Both businesspeople and journalists need to understand each other's needs [see sidebar "Can't We All Just Get Along (Starting Now)?"]. Of course, at the same time, you have to protect yourself. Ethical reporters, producers, and editors are the only ones to deal with. If you work with a reporter who "has it in for you" once, he'll be trouble the second, third, or tenth time. Just stay away from him.

As for the other 90 percent, go with your gut: If you have something to share, share it. If you're in a secretive state and *do not want the publicity,* but know that one day you might, try to steer the reporter to someone in your industry who might be willing to talk. Just don't spend all your time hemming and hawing—and don't think that not returning a call is the answer to dealing with the media.

Can't We All Just Get Along (Starting Now)?

Someone once told us that media people often dislike PR practitioners a lot. We don't see that, but then again, sometimes in the media industry it does seem as though the only time journalists and PR people get together is to point out how miserable the other is. There's a lot of love lost between the two forces, but the truth is, one can't exist well without the other.

The aim of public relations is to distribute information to the masses. Public companies have a responsibility to shareholders, customers, employees, and neighborhoods to tell these constituencies what's going on. PR practitioners make all of that happen. Conceptually, PR people were put on earth, or at least America, to put information out to the public and to be a resource to journalists.

The public relations profession has evolved from a consultant-as-needed model into a full-time gig. Companies, in some instances, have also made hiding information a major function of the role. This

Sure, there are people in the press who are just using you—and they'll put words in your mouth. Heck, your mom will do that, too. But pros are pros. Anyone worth his weight in the journalism world knows that he's not a fiction writer, creating strange and mysterious characters and fantastic tales of intrigue. Non-fiction is real life, and real life is messy and takes time to figure out. Good reporters know that.

That said, you need to be equally careful about what you put out there in the media. Passing on inaccurate or misleading information to make your story sound juicier is asking for trouble. Lots of it! Lies, even exaggerations and half-truths, always rise and bob around on the surface for all to see, especially in print. Reporters can go to any search engine and find out if you're making stuff up about partners, past deals, or anything else. Plus, they always have their ears to the ground. Decent reporters can scrutinize. They can

practice is really what marked the beginning of the rift between jour-
nalism and public relations. Big businesses have used PR to keep use-
ful and often damaging information under wraps.

From here, the job has escalated into using PR as a marketing tool
to spin just the glowing facts. This, in turn, compromises the integrity
of journalism and gives rise to the resentment that journalists feel
toward PR people in general. Can you say Enron?

Ultimately, the PR industry stands to benefit from some self-
regulation, watchdog organizations, and certification of some sort, a
development we'd love to see happen. The truth is, well, the truth: PR
people who hew to the facts are tending a landscape that is entirely
better for the PR industry.

On the flip side, journalists can get great ideas, find the help that
they need, and get connected to sources they want, need, and covet,
if they'd just give the PR guys a chance. Ah, working together. Our
kind of world.

We call that smart.

write letters. Make phone calls. Find out more about the slightest
whiff of fudge.

And if the reporter doesn't find you out, the thousands of
other people reading that story will. For example, take our
friends at the delivery logistics agency who get coverage for
trucking in supplies during an emergency. Once their story runs
on the evening news, all the other logistics consultants are going
to want their two cents heard. If the news story contains any inac-
curacies or misstatements, they won't hesitate to point it out.
Therefore, if you have not been straight with journalists in telling
your story, **they will hear about it**—mark our boldfaced words.
And you *will* be screwed.

Who Ya Gonna Get to Do the Dirty Work?

SINCE WE KNOW the pundits aren't ready to drive nails into your coffin, and they want to treat you as fairly as you *deserve,* how do you get them on the phone? You call! But before you pick up the phone, make sure you know which paper or magazine is the right one, and who is the best journalist to contact. Don't call people or e-mail them, asking, "Are you the right guy for this idea?"

Start by picking up the past ten issues of the newspaper or magazine to get more acquainted with it. *Do your homework.* Try to find the right journalist. One who is willing, if need be, to say, "I'm wrong for this. Sorry." Are they covering public companies? Are they columnists or reporters? For those who aren't sure of the precise difference ('fess up, now), columnists are people who write snippets of sometimes sinister, often salacious tidbits and news-of-the-second on people and places, peppered with their own opinions or outlooks. Reporters create stories of longer-lasting value, often with an interesting snippet or vignette leading off the story.

Once you've narrowed your search a bit, find out what your target reporter does. For example, does he specialize in profiles of public firms? Does he go for local neighborhood news, or does he only cover big-time entertainment muckety-mucks?

After you've found the right writer and you have his or her ear, tell the full story. Withholding important information makes for a poor story, or no story at all. Since we know it's not innate in journalists to inflict pain, we can rest a little easier knowing that everything doesn't have to be a secret, damaging, or, God forbid, proprietary. If you are honest with reporters, they will try hard to be fair with you.

Selling 'That There Story'

NOW THAT YOU ARE more comfortable with the idea of working with journalists, have the perfect angle, and have answered the age-old question, "Who ya gonna call?", how do you get it in the paper? You give that journalist exactly what he needs. Let's get back to the reporter's day and what is important to him. As we said, journalists are crushed for time, all the time, so if you can alleviate some of the pressure, they will thank you for it. Indeed.

How to Get, and Keep, the Reporter on the Phone

Consider the journalist's day. In fact, let's consider our friend Greg's day. He's a writer with News.com, one of the big websites for news. His job is to churn out two-and-a-half stories a day! That's a lot, especially when you consider he has to find the right angle for his audience, research the background, interview people, and then write the story.

Also, it's important to point out that the pressure is even greater with a Web news site. One of the benefits of sites like News.com is that they can report the news anytime, day or night, and are not confined to time-to-print. That said, to compete with the so-called papers of record, such as the *Los Angeles Times, Philadelphia Inquirer,* or *Washington Post,* to name a few, they have to report things as they are happening and get the scoop before these papers run it the next morning on the stands.

So what does that mean for Greg? It means that day in and day out, he must keep his ear to the rail, even more so than traditional reporters. There's the daily research on the Web to see what others are covering, a visit to Business Wire (see Chapter 9, "That Internet Chapter") to read the morning announcements, a roundup of Wall Street to see which companies are affecting the market, calls to trusted sources (like you, we imagine!) merely to find out the inside scoops and to stay on top of movers and shakers.

He has to read between the lines of every deal that is announced—most news in business involves partnerships—read the fine print in the general news, and spend hours on the phone trying his darndest to separate fact from fiction. And in the end, he still needs to actually write two-and-a-half stories a day before packing it in, just to come back the next day and do it all again.

Ah. It's a tough life. The combined pressures of so many demands push down on Greg with enough force to make his cubicle buckle. A PR pro knows enough to respect the position journalists are in. And by understanding how to release the pressure valve a bit, you become one of Greg's most trusted sources.

Matchmaker, Matchmaker...

But let's take a step back for a moment and start with the fundamental question behind journalist/story matchmaking: Why Greg? To answer that, we need to do some homework. Consider your story. Which audience are you after—and, by extension, which media outlet is geared to the same type of consumer as your customers? More specifically, who in the media will reach your target?

Greg's site covers technology business, so he and his 7 million readers with big budgets (the site's readers are mostly executives and other corporate decision makers) aren't going to give a darn about your new line of backpacks. But maybe you've embedded those backpacks with a global positioning system (GPS) and an avalanche beacon for cliffhangers and mountaineers. Some inventive circuitry brings your packs a little closer to Greg's place, but we still need to dig deeper to ensure this is the right fit. The major criteria are that the story has to be technology related, and it has to include some aspect of a Fortune 1000 firm.

Perhaps the GPS tracking systems stuffed in your knapsack utilize a new biotech application; maybe they can monitor some aspect of its wearer's health and give rescue teams a call should your body temperature drop or your blood pressure reach the sky. Yep, you have the beginnings of a tech story in the bag, and whenever you have circuitry making its way into what was formerly a simple aspect of life, you have a pretty compelling story for News.com.

But don't heave a sigh of relief yet: The story's still not bulletproof. Why should Greg cover a start-up manufacturer when 90 percent of new businesses sink as infants? Do we have any Fortune 1000 connections here? Is there some deal in the works that might affect a stock price or two—is the backpack the first tangible aspect of a whole new corporate strategy? Let's say, for conversation's sake, that your hiker gizmo was produced in part by Apple Computer, which bought into your textile company in an effort to expand its own innovative machinery beyond computers. There you go.

Any of these interesting, quirky angles make you legit in the eyes of Greg's news-gathering site. And yet there is still one more step! Is our buddy Greg the right writer for this innovation? He's not the only reporter at News.com.

To figure it out, let's flip through the past three months of his digital broadsheet. Like any journalist, he should show something consistent in all of his stories, and you can find that common thread by going online and searching the publication's digital archives. Perhaps he only writes about newly public companies or the venture capitalists that fund them. Maybe Greg covers West Coast businesses, e-commerce, or the government.

Then there's his reporting style. It is gossipy, or is it just a collection of news briefs? Perhaps he only produces executive profiles. Maybe he pulls together letter-like journal pieces. There are lots of choices here, and you can't sell him a story unless you know what he might be looking for.

After comparing a few of his pieces, you figure it out. Our man in News.com is, it appears, an editor for the e-business section, focusing on big companies and their new ideas and products. We have a hit—or the potential for one! Since we've read the past few months of his work, thanks to the Internet, we are sure he hasn't covered every GPS-stuffed ski pole and avalanche-foiling parka. If he had, our backpacks would be greeted with a yawn and a quick bye-bye.

Walk a Mile in His Shoes

So now we're into the pitch. We've confirmed that Greg is indeed the right person for the task. Now how do we go about convincing him to put aside all the other ideas and pitches he's received this morning to dedicate the next five hours of his life to our packs? At this stage you have already learned the number one lesson in PR: putting yourself in someone else's shoes. Getting Greg's attention with this professional approach doesn't equal ink just yet, however. Proceed with caution.

For example, now that you have Greg's ear—for fifteen seconds—don't steamroll him with a big sales pitch for which he has neither the time nor the interest. On the other hand, if you're going to call him with a pitch or an idea, don't do it halfway and leave it up to him to find the news angle inside. It's all in how you phrase it, but in general, if you respect Greg's time and needs, many of those two-and-a-half stories will go toward helping your cause.

Over the past couple of years, the New York Police Department has been doing a little PR of its own in an attempt to mend some seriously scorched bridges with the public. Now, just below the flashing lights and behind the back door where perpetrators file in and out, their patrol cars read "Courtesy, Professionalism, Respect." The slogan for CPR suggests the circle of respect that civilians should show the police, and vice versa, in order for everyone to work together.

CPR works in PR, too. When you get Greg on the phone, remember the two-point-five articles knocking on his door, and ask if he can spare a few minutes to hear about a story that's a custom fit for him, and him alone. If he doesn't have a moment, find a time that works better, and make sure you call back at the appointed hour. *Make a date.* Hanging up without one is as bad as leaving a voice mail. And leaving a voice mail is as bad as taking a nap.

As they say in show biz, give it all you got! Your enthusiasm and newfound familiarity with Greg's work will surely pique his interest (unless he's in a bad mood; then call back later), and he will somehow find a few minutes to listen to your shtick. This isn't the time to go into some formatted sales routine, because sales pitches that might work with regular people count for very little with journalists. No journalist wants to hear the exaggerated slant; it's an instant turn-off.

A quick but important detour: Remember CPR. We're up to the "P" part now. All together now: professionalism. Hard facts and concrete statistics win that coverage, not questionable numbers, hearsay, and spin doctoring. A journalist's job is based on reporting the facts. As we said before, and it bears repeating, don't make things up for the sake of getting your story in print. There's nothing worse than someone calling your bluff in print ("reading your beads" is our favorite expression). What's more, Greg, who trusted you, just got called on the carpet from his editor, and he's angry and embarrassed. You can be sure that he won't listen to your pitch again for a very long time, if ever.

It's All in the Follow-Through

Anyway, back to the job at hand. Greg liked the story; he bit. You cannot rest now. Don't hang up and start calling people or high-fiving your mate. Now the real work begins. Chances are, Greg's going to need to speak to someone else besides you. Sometimes it's an industry analyst (whom you've already lined up, right? If not, see Chapter 3, "Power Tools for Building Buzz") familiar with the clothing industry or a fashion technologist who's an expert on so-called wearable devices. Maybe you can give Greg the phone number of one of your investors, with that person's permission, naturally. Or someone who just likes you and your company's concept—say, for example, a contact you have at a local retailer (the Nike store?).

Our vote: Find someone who's survived an avalanche or who knows someone who went up with an ordinary backpack and never came back! If you don't happen to know any sherpas or Mount Everest veterans, get on the Web, check out the sites of a few adventure or mountaineering magazines, and find an account that'll make your point.

In addition to these sorts of accounts, known in PR as third-party validation, Greg is also going to need some hard data, such as when the packs are going to be available, how many you've sold to date, the cost, how many different models of the pack exist and what the differences are, and how the GPS component works. Do not speak to him like a techno geek or a nervous Nelly (sorry, Nelly). Just be forthright and anticipate. Have the info close at hand. If he asks a zinger that you can't answer or are uncomfortable answering right then and there, simply say, "Hey, I need to check on that and call you back."

Offer help. Tell him, and mean it, that there will be a sample pack at his desk first thing in the morning. Reporters love the word "overnight," and they are not referring to sleep-over parties. You could also e-mail him professional photos of the product or detailed documents that better explain the technology behind it all.

Professionalism is always about access. Once a journalist bites, you need to be there, close at hand, with whatever he's going to need—and you have to be fast. We can't stress enough the need for continuous follow-up. You must have ready all the materials Greg's going to need, eliminating a chunk of research time for him. Stats, past coverage, quotes, phone numbers of contacts, and the times the contacts are available are all valuable and necessary. Don't make him wait. Would you adore being kept waiting by someone who wants something very specific from you? Doubtful.

If the pitch has anything to do with your business, the number of an analyst familiar with the field and a summary of your business plan would be extremely helpful to Greg. This is a good way to ingratiate yourself with a media person with whom you hope to have a really long and wonderful relationship. It's also a good way for start-up operations to prove how you actually make money and if your business model seems good enough to support your great products and service.

And if there's someone else for Greg to speak to at your company, get that person ready. If your coworker, no matter how high up she is, says she isn't available, your job is to make her available. If she has a prior commitment, suggest that she postpone it for an hour. In the movie *Cast Away,* a pre-stranded Tom Hanks drives into his Russian-based FedEx colleagues that their competitor is the clock. Live and die by this advice if you're doing PR for yourself.

In short, access is a journalist's friend, so give Greg access to everything—information, yourself, and your time. That can sometimes seem impossible, given the demands of your day, but you can manage it. We always tell people that you can talk to the journalist for a few seconds or minutes, but that if it's anything more than a quick quote or help with background information, reschedule the discussion for sometime in the early evening or first thing the next morning, whatever is easiest for you. It's crucial to block enough time to work with him, or any other journalist, so he can find the best part of the story with you.

You've come a long way at this point toward getting the press coverage you need, but just because Greg or any other journalist shows an initial interest, you're not guaranteed space on the site or wherever their work lands. You need to mold his work—

help him write the piece. We are not saying you have to "make the words appear" (we can't tell you how many people still think PR people *write* the stories), just keep the dialogue going. Don't let him get sidetracked.

Most reporters really appreciate your wanting the story to happen. If it's a good enough story, then of course you're going to make sure he follows through with it. That's to be expected. Media professionals who say, "Leave me alone" will find themselves awfully lonely in the near future. News has a shelf life. Therefore, if you don't keep pace with your favorite journalist, Greg, well, before you know it, he'll move on to his next story. As a final check, go over all the information with him to ensure that what he's reporting is really correct.

The Emily Post School of Media Manners

OKAY, SO YOU'VE DONE a good job, and you've respected the journalist's ethics, job, and requirements. What should you expect in return? Nothing less than the same respect you've shown him. You should also expect a long working relationship out of this successful encounter. Smart journalists will take note of good contacts and put them into their special Rolodexes. It's not often that a source impresses them. (See Chapter 7 for more on the source-filing concept.)

What if you've shown that respect to the reporter, and it's not returned in kind? After all of your hard work, if you are maligned or treated impolitely with no justification, remove that person's name from your database. Your life's too short, and the bad attitude would probably carry over to the story, anyway! We know reporters are busy—and you're bored with us saying that—and yes, they field a lot of unwanted calls (yawn), but this does not give them the right to be rude or uncivil.

When you *are* happy with an introduction and story process, always send a handwritten thank-you note, letting the journalist

Five Ways to a Reporter's Heart

1 *Be courteous. Understand the media's job and treat journalists with respect.*
2 *Do your homework.*
3 *Never exaggerate.*
4 *Don't ever—ever—lie.*
5 *Always follow up as promised immediately.*

know how much you appreciate the productive back-and-forth. Top it off with a business card and a note listing all of the related projects you're working on (the next generation of your backpack, for instance, or cold-weather gear that senses impending frostbite and sends out an alarm). Mention other upcoming products or services, or things you "forgot" to mention during the interview. It's like leaving a scarf or a sock after a first date. It's a reason to return.

This way, when Greg is facing a looming deadline again and is casting about for a source of information, he knows exactly how you can and can't help ... and if you add a note with fun story notions on it, you might get a call from him, asking you to "tell me about that idea, again." We call that good media relations and good business.

The last thing we need to tell you about how the press really works is a simple rule most people would never think of. *Be playful.* That does not mean minimizing the subject at hand, and we're not suggesting that you have to become bosom buddies with a journalist, but you can be one of the nicer people he has to deal with in his day. What did your mom tell you? Say something nice. They'll remember. Amen.

PART II

The Nitty-Gritty

CHAPTER 3

Power Tools for Building Buzz

TACTICS ARE THE ACTIONS and activities that help you attain the goals of your strategy, the "how to" section of any media plan. Characterize it any way you like—nuts and bolts, nitty-gritty, meat and potatoes—it's the foundation you need to build up buzz. Although tactics take many forms, from straightforward to straight out of the asylum, they all have one thing in common: creativity. Whatever your battle strategy, go to it blazing with flair and innovation, and deploy your plan with a sense of confidence and importance.

For every situation, you can make use of any number of tactics to brilliantly publicize (or downplay) an event. And don't fall into the one-size-fits-all trap: If you're trying to reach multiple audiences, organize a separate set of tactics for each one. Here's a broad array of essential tools and approaches you need to consider to start raising some buzz for yourself.

Analyst Meetings

For companies that are public or aspiring to go public, analyst meetings are those in which executive members of the company discuss their strategy, finances, and investments with research analysts well-versed in that company's industry or sector. From the PR perspective, a well-conducted meeting will produce three outcomes:

❑ An analyst who is often contacted by the media will be able to discuss your business knowledgeably and thus generate press for you.

❑ Equally important, he or she will become a credible third-party endorsement.

❑ Plus, analysts can make constructive suggestions on the business model you present and put you in touch with potential business partners.

It's a good idea to have a PowerPoint-type presentation available for the analysts. This is a take-home document, so distribute it toward the end of the meeting to ensure that the analysts are paying attention to your oral presentation and not reading ahead of or behind you. Make sure it's neat, clear, and well organized, and in general presents a professional image of your company.

The documents, as well as the presenters meeting with the analysts, should be prepared to withstand severe scrutiny. Needless to say, the content of your slides is more important than the graphic artistry. Review the slides over and over, making sure that the story they tell is clear and compelling. Remember, industry analysts aren't telling investors what to buy and what to sell, as much as they're reporting on your company's state of the union, including, where relevant, any advancement of technology. Proprietary information should be referenced as appropriate. Analysts will respect secrets, and if your scheme depends on that special technology or algorithm the company has created, let them in on it to the extent possible. Once your materials are ready, get yourself in presentation shape, too. Practice your own presentation and pay attention to the overall order and flow of the presentations of others. Determine who says what, and go through a rehearsal or two together. You might consider inviting someone who knows a thing or two about your industry to sit in on a dry run of the presentation and poke holes in it before an analyst does. Most important, know your company's weaknesses; explain how the company is prepared to address them, going forward. Analysts want to know that you've considered the worst and have a game plan in place.

Choose the analyst firms you meet with carefully. You should be meeting with the experts in your field. After meeting with the analysts, keep them up-to-date with the company's ongoing activities. If they know what's happening with your company, they will be more likely to speak to the press about you. Send press releases on subjects such as updates on technology, a quarterly summary of new clients signed or distribution outlets opened, and so on. Don't clutter an analyst's inbox with an update of every little detail, just major milestones. Contrary to popular wisdom, too much is, in fact, too much.

If you feel an analyst is impressed with your presentation, give that individual's contact information to journalists, at selected times and with the analyst's permission, of course. As with sending updates, this, too, should be done sparingly and with kid gloves. But if you do have an opportunity to speak with a major press outlet like the Associated Press or *Time,* an analyst can offer some weighty, third-party validation to your claims.

Beta or Product Testing

Beta testing is a stage in the corporate development of a product. Before releasing a product to the public, the company gives it to selected consumers and/or journalists for testing and a sneak peak. This is a tactic that works especially well for hardware manufacturers, and it can have useful media results. By allowing journalists to participate, you create the potential for some excellent press coverage. Assuming your product stands up to the testing, the journalist should submit a glowing product review.

Of course, this means being fairly certain that you've worked most of the bugs out of the product. It should be far along in its development stage, and in both form and function it should be as close as possible to the final version.

To arouse interest in your beta test, send a personalized letter to all of the appropriate reporters who review products for your industry, inviting them to try the product before the public is able to purchase or use it. Include a high-resolution photo with the product. That way, if the reporter decides to review your product, she'll already have a good photo of it. Once again, you've just made her life easier.

Inviting journalists into a beta test is most useful when you're trying to get coverage in stories they're already working on. If the *Los Angeles Times* technology writer is working on a story about wireless phone technology and you are beta-testing your new WAP (wireless application protocol) phone, then let her participate in the beta test. Just make sure she understands that the last few bugs still need to be worked out.

Before engaging journalists in a beta test, double-check that the product or service will be available to consumers by the agreed-upon date. If reporters include a product mention in a story, they want to make sure the availability information is accurate. It's best to keep launch dates flexible, but it's better to say something will be available in early spring, as compared to April 10.

Projected days and times are tough to hold to, and you don't want to look as if you've missed your own launch date. Once you've pinpointed a more accurate date (within two weeks or so of the actual launch), contact all the journalists to whom you've spoken in the past and alert them to the big day.

Finally, send a final version of the product or service to everyone who participated in the beta test. This often leads to a follow-up story. Or, if the journalist has been sitting on the story, he may decide it's time for your product to see ink.

B-Roll

A B-roll is flattering video footage that a company produces to complement a news release. Broadcast news services often use the provided B-roll for background in their story and then lay the audio of their broadcast over the video. You can also use a B-roll for live broadcasts. When producing a B-roll, have copies made in different formats. Most news stations still rely on beta tapes, which have become the standard in the industry, but others are moving toward digital equipment, and DVD footage is favored.

A well-produced B-roll will show the product or service being used in its intended setting. For example, a company that produces wireless headsets for cell phones would produce a B-roll showing mobile users en masse, uncomfortably holding phones to their ear (or smashing their cars), quickly followed by a group of people using the wireless headset, looking relaxed and happy as they stroll or drive along.

Typically, a B-roll is silent video, and most of the time, news stations won't use a reel with text and promotional babble on it. Keep it clean and make sure that the visual illustrates your message through action.

Send interested broadcast news producers a copy of the footage in advance so they can spend the time needed to work it into the piece they are editing without having the pressure of the clock. Again, make a quick call to check which format their studio requires.

Don't try to borrow your brother's video camera and do this yourself. A B-roll producer is easy to find and can be located in the yellow pages under camera operators. You can distinguish the pros from the amateurs by asking what type of equipment they use to shoot. VHS is a no-no, whereas three-bit digital is a plus, because it can be converted to almost anything.

Also, quiz them on their creative approach to the piece. If they're leaving all the ideas up to you and not providing any professional insight of their own, you should shop elsewhere. B-roll production can be costly, but shouldn't total more than $8,000 or $9,000 from concept to duplication of the final product.

Crisis Management

Your preparation for the unexpected is otherwise known as Plan B. It's every company's worst public relations nightmare—the accidental distribution of contaminated food, a delivery truck crash, sinking a Greenpeace boat—you name it. The goal is to be nimble and proactive and to get your positive message out there quickly.

Contrary to what you might think, someone other than the CEO or designated spokesperson can address negative situations. An apology, explanation, or what appears like defensive maneuvering from the CEO will deteriorate the branding among investors and other audiences. It's best to use a less-senior executive, such as a vice president, to deliver the message. In a crisis, it isn't so much who says it, but what's said. It's a time of quotes and sound bites, and the media will listen to any senior executive, as long as she's willing to answer tough questions.

When the story first makes the news, never hide from the situation, but try not to take the blame, either. It is usually safe to say, "We are looking into the situation," or "We are on the alert and will keep you informed as we learn more."

Also, keep things positive and never alienate potential partners or customers. In the case of upended Fords and flimsy Firestone tires, both companies publicly pointed the finger at each other, resulting in a public tit-for-tat that didn't alleviate the fears of *any* consumers. Name calling will only come back to haunt you in the end. It's best to say that you are investigating the problem; stake out the moral high ground by playing the role of the great avenger, the one who will bring order to things. Statements such as, "It is our goal to provide the best products and services to our consumers, and we work with them and related consumer groups daily on these two fronts to make sure we do so" and "We are working hand in hand with (the police, someone's family, etc.) to correct the situation in these three ways" are action-oriented and positive, while still acknowledging the gravity of the situation.

Since you can never predict the timing of a crisis, it's important to have messages on hand at all times that can quickly be relayed to the media, if necessary. Try to consider the worst-case scenario. This might be a fatal accident caused by an intoxicated driver of your company behind the wheel if you own a trucking company, or children being injured in your (as it turns out) not-so-safe safety seat. Write the problems down, as well as all of the possible questions such an event would generate, and put these into a file. Of course, if the hypothetical seems more real than hypothetical, you need to fix it, but that's beyond the scope of this book.

From there, think long and hard about the right answers to the tough questions. You need answers that will paint you as action oriented and positive and that best minimize the negative impact on your business.

Embargo

Many journalists like to have information before other media outlets do for any number of reasons: Some break only exclusive stories, others have long lead times, and so on. An embargo is the act of giving the necessary information to a journalist beforehand, with the understanding that he will not release the information before an agreed-upon date.

Embargos are most useful when you want information to hit the news with strategic timing, while dealing with multiple lead times and news media. In order for an interested journalist at a weekly magazine to compete with an online news outlet, he needs the information early, as it can take up to three weeks to make it to the news racks.

The news you are announcing must be ready and fit for the presses before you offer the embargo. Anything can happen, both internally and externally, but if the information becomes invalid or changes, that journalist will not be happy. The trick is to enter into an embargo only with news that you consider certain. If you're launching a new product in a month, make sure it's finished, debugged, and ready to sell. Offer the embargo to the right journalist and then take your contraption, put it in the vault, and speak nothing of it until your agreed-upon date. Until that time, mum's the word. In a world where everyone has a website and news travels fast, any sort of leak will get back to that reporter, and you'll have an angry person with the means to influence others on your hands.

Use embargoes wisely. Offering an embargo to a journalist will demonstrate that you are an experienced PR pro and will place you in the good graces of that publication. Offering embargoes and following through with them is the fastest way to build solid working relations with journalists. On the flip side, giving an embargo and then taking it away midstream is the fastest way to get blackballed by a publication.

Events

There are various creative activities to further build buzz. Events take many forms, ranging from launch parties and panel discussions to webcasts or even competitions.

Compare the event's cost to the potential buzz you can generate. That's not always as simple as it seems. For example, elaborate launch parties often result in only a small amount of off-message press, while an inexpensive activity or stunt can generate a huge response and illustrate exactly what a company is all about. The best events are visual, creative, and unique, and they offer a new approach to a familiar situation. An example of a potentially inexpensive and effective event would be to gather the nation's fastest typists in a major city, such as Los Angeles, and then let them compete against a voice-recognition product. Then you can publicize the fact that your technology takes the title.

Another criterion to keep in mind for events is location, location, location. Everyone wants to go places that either are trendy or on their list of places to visit. For the launch of the first online city guide in 1995, we chose the top of the World Trade Center towers, Windows on the World, because (we now look back wistfully) that was a short time after it had been reopened. We knew that the restaurant wanted a party there, and reporters were anxious to see the new post-1993 top of the towers.

But even if you don't have anything that exciting in your town as the venue for your event, it's your job to create atmosphere. Do you have a famous or unusual museum with a garden? A historical center? Perhaps a well-known poet from the 1800s lived in a certain rooming house in your town, and it's now accessible as a cultural party domain. Or you could *cheat* and just go to the pub where the poet did his drinking!

Launch parties can really be a drag for you *and* the attendees. If you don't make it exciting and fun, no one will come. And don't forget you have to make good on whatever you promise. For example, a local New York magic show that specializes in mentalism (otherwise known as reading minds) wanted to expand its audience. Around that time, a celebrity magician with a budget had publicized his claim that anyone who could deduce his secret (or even stump him) would win $10,000 and the magician's Jaguar. So the little magic show devised its own contest, live and free to the press, naturally. The point of the contest was to tell everyone that if they could figure out how any of the show's feats were done, they'd win a token and a bagel! This being downtown New York, everyone in the media laughed. Not everyone came, but plenty of journalists covered this anti-big-hype idea. Suddenly, the event became secondary to the joke, but it still garnered its fair share of press coverage.

Even with small events like this one, costs can pile up fast. Get a strong handle on all of the potential expenses before you go ahead. Our advice about parties will upset party planners. Unless you can get some sort of major sponsor (local restaurants or alcohol manufacturers usually will do it if you can promise press and due credit), a party should be simple and effective. If you're trying to get people to network, for example, you still need to provide food and hors d'oeuvres for your cocktail party, but you can focus your energies on finding fresh ways for people to connect, rather than on conspicuous consumption.

That said, don't neglect the logistical aspects. Invite the media with plenty of advance notice. Keep in mind that the average positive response is about 5 percent, so if you want forty people to come to your event, send out 800 invitations. A week after you've sent out the invitations, follow up with reminder calls and collect RSVPs. One more "we know you're coming" reminder is very important. Do it even if you think this is over the top, because people do forget.

Finally, choose the day and time wisely. Events can be a success on Tuesday and a failure on Friday. Many weekly journalists and columnists have a Wednesday deadline, making their days unavailable but their evenings free. Evening events are typically better attended earlier in the week, as social calendars tend to conflict on Thursdays and Fridays. Mondays are horrible for getting TV coverage in major cities. News teams just cannot get a crew to commit to an event over a weekend, and on Monday, everyone starts planning their week. If you want TV coverage, avoid it.

If possible, check to see if any other newsworthy events are occurring at the same time as yours. If they are, change the date if you can. Picking a slow media day increases your chances of media turnout. Yes, you read that right: You *want* a slow news day. If other exciting (or even not so exciting) things are happening, you'll get excuses from everyone, especially anyone who counts.

Exclusive

A tactic similar to an embargo (discussed previously), an exclusive is an agreement that you make to allow a certain journalist to run your story first. Just as you're competing with other companies in your industry and other PR pros to get ink in the *Wall Street Journal,* journalists compete to break a story first. Many publications, such as News.com or the *San Jose Mercury News,* for example, opt not to run the story at all if they aren't breaking it first.

But giving an exclusive is tricky. First, you have to pin down the target audience and the news hook for the story. If you're making a corporate announcement designed to strengthen your company's position in the Web industry, then break it in the *San Jose Mercury News.* This is indeed where your peers will read it and weep. If you're introducing the greatest new gadget to help golfers find their balls in the rough, then place it in *Golf Weekly,* or even *Forbes ASAP,* the *Forbes* supplement that executives read and relish.

Do not offer an exclusive to a long-lead magazine, because it might take six weeks to run, and by then your news will be old. Also, it may not be the best place for a story you think is big. Always check with the editor first to determine the approximate lead time for both feature articles and regular departments and columns.

What's the difference between exclusives and embargos? An embargo is really a type of exclusive, one that must be held for certain internal reasons, such as investor or SEC requirements, or a pending deal that requires an embargo on the news. As with an embargo, tread carefully with an exclusive, and be as certain as you can that your news will unfold as you planned.

If you do decide to give a journalist an exclusive, spread the wealth and consider noncompeting outlets. That means positioning your news for several different audiences, so you can grant an exclusive to each publication without stepping on any toes. For example, it is definitely acceptable to give *USA Today* the exclusive that golfers can find your new golf ball in the rough, thanks to a satellite chip in its center, and how the company plans to profit from its magic ball. At the same time, you could grant a mag like *eWeek* a simultaneous interview that focuses on how the technical wizardry works.

You don't need to tell either magazine the content of the other's exclusive (in fact, you shouldn't). However, it's important to let both journalists know that you're giving a related story to a noncompetitive outlet—in this case, that you're talking with both a daily and a technology-driven magazine. Chances are they won't care about each other.

The exclusive should work in your favor and be worth the trade-off (the inability to pitch the story to other competing publications). Sometimes publicists have turned down good print opportunities to secure an "exclusive" story with a particular publication only to find out that the article runs as a three-line mention. Before offering a journalist an exclusive on a story, find out the subject and angle of the story and how much coverage you can reasonably expect.

Once your exclusive has seen the light of day, keep the momentum going. Use your time wisely; don't wait too long after the exclusive has run to start pitching other media. You don't want to make everyone else feel as if they're two steps lower on the media food chain. In many cases, press coverage is its own validation. A reporter from a major weekly seeing the story in a minor weekly now understands it from his brethren's point of view. Likewise, seeing the story in a major weekly makes trade reporters sit up and really take notice.

In-Person Interview

Interviews are always best conducted in person. Speaking to reporters over the phone and online does not make for great connections; you form relationships only once you've met someone. That's why having a brief meeting over coffee or a stand-up discussion is so much more engaging than just one more phone call in the litany of dozens in a journalist's day-to-day grind. It's a simple truth, but it is a truth. Here are some basic tips to make your interview successful (advanced users, please read Chapter 6 for more detailed instructions).

❑ **Before you go to the interview**—in fact, before you even agree to it—you should fully understand the journalist's angle for the article. Conversely, the journalist should understand exactly what your company does. Any confusion or misunderstandings on either side will lead to an awkward interview and a potentially unflattering story.

❑ **Go to the interview thoroughly prepped.** Prepare a list of speaking points and answers to potential questions. You might even want to read some past articles the journalist has written, so you can get a feel for the reporter's style beforehand.

❑ **Bring any relevant supporting material with you to the interview.** This includes your most recent press release, a fact sheet, headshots, a press kit, and perhaps even a laptop. You should give the journalist a sheet with all your contact information—your phone, beeper, and cell phone numbers, and your e-mail address. Your contact sheet should also display your name, exactly as you'd like to see it in print, as well as your title and your company's proper name.

❑ **If the interview revolves around your product, bring a live demo with you, if possible.** Stay away from canned demos if you have a live Internet product or software or hardware, because they're exactly that—canned and unimpressive. Finally, the day before the meeting, send a message to the journalist to remind him of the meeting and to double-check that it's on his schedule.

Leak

Information can be given to the media in an anonymous fashion. It's a sneaky but often-used tactic that lets companies expose weaknesses in the competition by starting a strategic, and often unconfirmed, rumor best not associated with the source.

Rosie O'Donnell once recounted on the *Today* show how word of her lover's pregnancy was leaked to the media. She walked out of the doctor's office, delirious with joy. An older woman asked if everything was okay. Rosie replied, "I'm so happy—we're pregnant." That woman happened to be the mother of a national magazine editor. Well, that's a leak.

Only leak information that you really want to put out there. Releasing protected information can land you in trouble, so make sure the journalist with whom you are speaking is prepared to conceal your identity. In a normal run-in with the media, you never say anything off the record. Here, however, you are giving them usable information but concealing the source. If they want it badly enough, they'll follow the rules. But you need to follow them, too. The journalist has decided to trust you and your leak, so make sure the information you are releasing is factual, newsworthy, and not based on speculation.

By the same token, carefully choose the outlet to which you leak information. You should choose a daily or weekly publication for the freshest and most timely press coverage. If the news has a closely held expiration date, stay away from the trades—they usually can't run something quickly. Also, if it's a trade story, chances are their writers will steer clear from slamming anyone who might be a potential or current advertiser.

Don't think that hot news is leakable if it's unethical or illegal to divulge it or if there's any way in which it can hurt you or your company's reputations. You might have a fantastic deal pending, one that you're contractually bound to shut up about until it's signed. Even if you are not officially attached to the news, the other company's lawyers will phone you. If a leak is traced back to you, you're screwed. Before you muster up the courage and phone number of the go-to journalist for the pitch, consider those involved. Are they lawyer-happy, or do they just need a good push? Think long and hard about that one before you proceed.

Despite the obvious dangers, leaks can help you get people off the fence, so to speak. For example, a large Internet company was holding for ransom an online product that really belonged to another, smaller Internet company. It refused to sign a deal that had ostensibly been agreed upon. A strategically placed leak informed the press that the large company was stalling. The next day, the deal was signed, sealed, and delivered.

Media Tour

A media tour involves taking your product, company, or idea on the road to present it to the media in regions that are strategically important for your business. These tours are often done for new product launches, or to announce milestones that a company has reached, such as its first million dollars in sales, ten years in business, and so on.

A media tour works well for companies or services that are region-specific. Local media are always more interested in stories that relate to their readers geographically, so if you have a story about a service that is available to them exclusively, or a company creating new jobs in their region, you stand a better chance of making it onto their pages.

Since you don't have unlimited time and resources, be selective about the type of coverage you want and choose the region accordingly. For example, most of the Internet trade press is based in the San Francisco region, much of the business press is centered in New York, and a majority of the telecom technology press is located in Boston.

What if you don't know which region is best? If it's your business, chances are you read the general trade magazines! Check the magazines themselves or their websites for addresses. If you're not even sure of that, go to your local Barnes & Noble or a decent newsstand and buy all the magazines related to your industry. Print magazines help twofold: You can check out the who, where, and what of the magazines, and you'll also get a feel for the writing and the type of articles they're looking for.

RLM took on pharmaceutical companies (and the trade news that covers them) in 2001, then a relatively new industry for us. The first thing we did was go to our favorite search engine, WiseNut, and search for any ocular (eye medicine) publications. We found three of the four worth going to. Plus, we called doctors ourselves and asked them what publications came to their house. It helped us get a basic handle on the industry.

Once you've narrowed down your target publications, start planning your media tour, albeit no more than a month in advance, because you won't have firm agreements for meetings until the day before. Buy the tickets and go. It's not necessary to have a general press conference of any sort. The idea is to be more fluid about what you will be doing in each city. But with that in mind, always let reporters know that you are only in town that day.

After you book the media tour and your individual meetings with reporters, you or your communications person must send all the necessary information well before the meeting. This should include a press kit, the most recent press release, the URL to your website (you do have a website, right?), and short biographies of people they'll be meeting. A fact sheet with all the important figures is helpful, too—revenue, number of employees, date company started, and so on.

Who should go? Only those people who are needed to say something—never more than two. You don't need more than one PR person in the room during a press meeting. But it is useful to have one, to ensure that people know why they're there and the focus of the meeting, and to keep everyone on track, rather than jabbering on about the weather.

The spokesperson's role is to drive home a particular message about your company while answering questions. But bear in mind that the only items that make it into print are conversations that are mutually beneficial. In other words, remember that the journalist is looking for a viable story for the audience. Therefore, if you talk only about your message and don't address the journalist's informational needs, your vapor and puffery will never see the light of day in print, no matter how many smiles that reporter offers you.

In general, interesting activities always draw media attention, and this holds true for a media tour, too. Prepare an interesting hook or stunt that's relevant to each city you are visiting. The importance of linking the product to the region cannot be stressed enough. For example, in many cities the Sci-Fi channel was able to scare the wits out of people, in a comical way, as it branched out to new markets in the mid-1990s. In our stomping ground, New York, Sci-Fi's gimmick was simple and notorious: It produced printed graphics of alligators on the street arising from under sewer caps. Since this is an "urban legend" in the streets of Manhattan, the gators hit home and really intrigued people enough to make them start watching the upstart channel.

As everyone knows, the Internet bubble went "pop" in 2000. In keeping with the new, more sober times, E*TRADE, which had amassed thousands of users and massive name recognition on the Web, needed to change its image from online stock-swapping facilitator to all-encompassing financial services firm. To do that, it decided to go ape with a media tour.

A year later, E*TRADE was advertising in the Super Bowl

with an infamous chimp for the third straight year. Not only was the ad meant to be a star of the game, as it had been in years past, but it was also going to introduce the world to E*TRADE's new image and brand expansion. The E*TRADE chimp was used as a device to build hype and anticipation for the upcoming Super Bowl ads. The chimp was chaperoned on a "photo celebration tour" of New York, where he was photographed at several New York City landmarks. The photos were then sent to the media to create pre-Super Bowl buzz and to tease reporters with the news that E*TRADE would be making a big announcement on the day of the Super Bowl.

Press Conference

A press conference is a staged forum in which journalists are invited to hear and witness a news announcement being made firsthand. A press conference is also the perfect mechanism to announce something important to a number of journalists, both print and broadcast, simultaneously.

Press conferences are tricky. You are asking someone who doesn't even leave his desk for a bagel to schlep somewhere that may be hard to find and to listen to you for two hours when he could be sitting across from you at his comfy conference table.

But don't despair. With a good hook, a conference can generate tremendous buzz. You need to do something truly original and different to entice journalists away from their busy work schedules to hear what you have to say. One surefire hook is a celebrity. Journalists will always come to see a known personality and take a photo with them—a living, breathing visual.

If you can't find a celebrity, do the next best thing: Devise a powerful way to deliver your message, preferably visually. Consider the following case study. In 2000, StarBand Communications, a high-speed, satellite Internet service, had been operating in "stealth" mode for more than a year, in order to develop its satellite technology behind closed doors. At that time, cable modems and DSL (digital subscriber line) owned the consumer market for quick connections amongst consumers in general and, more specifically, bandwidth "fiends."

According to the media, these two technologies were the answers to a surfer's prayers. Unfortunately, more than 50 million households lie outside a wire's reach, however. The idea behind the press conference, therefore, was to make an immediate media splash for StarBand by letting journalists (and, by extension, readers/consumers) know how limited the competing modes of DSL and cable access truly are.

To attract the consumer Internet market before the cable and DSL coverage had a chance to spread, StarBand's launch had to be big—and it was. A large press briefing was organized in Washington, D.C., StarBand's headquarters, where StarBand not only lifted the curtain on its satellite system but also showed the media just how incomplete broadband penetration had been to date. An oversized digital display shattered the high-speed myth by presenting a map of the United States, clearly identifying how limited broadband's reach actually is. Most of the United States was dark, until the satellite image lit up the rest of the country, bringing StarBand coast-to-coast and everywhere in between.

Just in case the media were still a little skeptical, StarBand brought in Sally Tilousi, a representative of the Havasupai tribe living in the Grand Canyon, where radio doesn't even reach. Ms. Tilousi explained how she uses StarBand technology to teach the tribe's children in school—before, the closest Internet connections were eight hours away—and how the police station and village hall were using dishes to tap into outside resources as well. Within forty-eight hours, articles about the press conference began appearing in dozens of both technology and general-interest publications.

What are other ways to shine? Community connections are one way to assure that local (and often national) reporters will visit your conference. Donate your product to an appropriate and appreciative organization, for example. When Polaroid invented the first-ever desk printer to make instant, photo-quality prints in 1998, it donated all of the first models to the Boston police for quicker "perp" identification and publicized this generous donation with a press conference. Technology journalists might not have understood the value, but Boston's local and city hall press got in the mood quickly; for them, this was something new and interesting.

Also think about bringing in information that reporters might learn from. For instance, a big draw at press events is showcasing well-known speakers in your industry—third-party validators. They will give a framework to the news that you're bringing to the press and answer reporters' questions. It's an endorsement from someone who speaks your language—and the journalists' language, too.

Be different in a different place. Unique locations are a media draw because they make for a much livelier background. For example, suppose the Transit Authority of the City of New York was announcing wired subways with high-speed Internet access. Why conduct the press conference in a faceless hotel conference facility when it could crank up the buzz by having it on one of the networked trains?

Now that you have some ideas about how to get the media flocking to your press conference, you need to get down to the nitty-gritty (sorry). The best way to book a press conference is to send out a media alert. This is something like a press release, but much shorter. It should say who, what, where, why, and when. It should also mention whether there will be a photo opportunity, and it should include your contact information, should anyone have questions. The media alert should be sent out to the media the day before the event and followed up by phone to encourage attendance.

Send your alert via e-mail, wire service, fax, and carrier pigeon. Each journalist has a preferred way of receiving news, so leave nothing to chance. When it comes to calling and following up, the more people you have working the phones, the better. A good PR person calls seventy people a day, if the list is relevant and the pitch second nature. If you are a one-man show, however, don't sweat it. Get a good chair, grab a drink of water, and dial for dollars.

As a final tip here, remember that the way to the media's heart is through its (collective) stomach. Order snacks, and let everyone know lunch will be served. It sounds simple, and it is! Simple human nature.

Press Kit

A press kit is a collection of materials that contain all the necessary background information on you and your company that journalists need to write a comprehensive article. Let's run through the important elements.

❑ **First we have the company backgrounder.** This should give information about the services or products the company provides, why the products are important and noteworthy, and the markets in which the company competes.

❑ **The fact sheet is next.** This is a one-page sheet with bullet points that highlight the key facts about your company: the full address, whether it is public or private, when it was established, how many employees it has, how much money has been raised (or if it's an older venture, any recent financial announcements or client deals), and a brief description of the service or product.

❑ **The kit should also include brief biographies** of the founders and/or executive management team. These descriptions allow journalists to better understand the executives' professional background and the management strengths they bring to the company.

❑ **Press releases are another important element.** Use all the major press releases that you've distributed in the past few months, and perhaps one or two milestone releases in the past year. These inform reporters about milestones in the company's history and help them develop a larger, more in-depth picture of the company.

❑ **Articles are crucial to the press kit.** Therefore, include a few news clips that explain different facets of the company. But don't go overboard; limit the number of clips to four. Too many articles might work against you and discourage a journalist from writing. That is, a journalist who sees a stack of newspaper and magazine articles might conclude that you've had plenty of exposure already and that any article he wrote wouldn't be newsy. That's not the message you want to convey.

❑ **Graphics or visuals help round out your story** for reporters by giving them an understanding of the product's form, as opposed to the function you've so gorgeously described. Always aim for high-resolution photos (digital is preferred) of your product, because reproducible quality increases the chances they'll use it in an article.

Press kits should always be on hand and available to questioning reporters at any kind of event, such as a press conference or media tour. But it's also a good idea to periodically mail kits with a pitch letter to targeted journalists. Even if you're not of immediate interest to them, they'll often file interesting stories and save them for a rainy day (one with no news in it).

Press Release

A press release is the backbone of any corporate news announcement, the document that will either entice or turn away a reporter. It's a standard written announcement distributed to the media that clearly announces information you wish to place in the news. The most successful releases are written very much like a story, and include the pitch, the necessary background information, and an interesting news hook.

It goes without saying (or perhaps it doesn't) that the news you are announcing should actually be newsworthy. A vapor release—one with no news of substance—will garner only unfocused news coverage. That doesn't help your cause at all. Plus, journalists will learn not to rely on you for "real" news.

The best way to translate your press release into a newspaper or magazine article is to target the journalists who will find the news most interesting and send the news release to them personally, with a pitch letter crafted to address their audiences' informational needs, as well as the journalist's particular news beat. And by the way, if you can avoid the press release, then *just pitch it.*

Surveys

Surveys can be a cheap and effective tool. Surveys of any kind are a great boon to magazines and newspapers, such as *USA Today,* that love to report on facts like "50 percent of us are eating more mayonnaise." And surveys are easy to do ... trust us.

A company we'll call Fungible produced downloadable audio versions of books, magazines, theater, and so on onto portable machines that allowed you to listen at home or in cars. For them RLM devised a simple-to-enact survey that polled 1,000 users on their favorite celebrity voices to listen to. Talk about an angle: It's all Hollywood, all the time. If you can't locate a celebrity tack, go over to the dark side, Luke: a survey on the worst problems one faces, for instance, when dealing with a telephone service rep. You can devise brief, simple surveys yourself, but for more complicated endeavors, it's probably worthwhile to use a market research professional, who will have expertise in survey methodology.

Trend Story

A trend story is a story pitch that encompasses more than just a particular announcement. It investigates recent developments in an entire market or industry. Trend stories are generally culture stories about what we commonly refer to as cultural phenomena. These are the type of stories that look at an emerging, newly social trend and wind up influencing those not yet in the know to follow suit. It's the way movements in business, fashion, and art—you name it—start. If you are part of a trend story, the media—and thus consumers—perceive you to be at the top of your game. Once you begin appearing in culture stories frequently, the public starts remembering your name, and sales become a breeze. Trend stories make more detail-oriented journalists take note. They will latch onto you and answer your queries faster because suddenly you're a "name."

This may all seem time-consuming, but the truth is that a trend story is what the journalists in weekly or monthly business magazines want most. Their publications don't move as quickly as the daily news, and information gets old quickly.

Coveted trend stories closely examine an aspect of "the story of the season." Consider the following hypothetical example. Wireless has been a hot market, and a great trend story for a magazine like *Fast Company* would be how local content through wireless devices is changing the shopping habits of young consumers, or how Western companies are using Japan as a test market for future technologies.

Before pitching a trend story, arm yourself with ample statistics and information about all of the major players in your market or industry, not just your company. The more data you can provide, the more likely the story will run. Naturally, there's nothing to stop a journalist from deciding that one of the other companies in the story is more interesting than yours, but that's just a risk you have to accept.

Video News Releases and Satellite Media Tours

Video news releases and satellite media tours are related strategies that are used similarly. Video news releases are undoubtedly much cheaper than satellite media tours, but they are both good tactics to consider, depending on your needs. A VNR is a taped video announcement that is distributed to multiple broadcast outlets. Prominent public corporations or politicians use this technique when they need to address many people across multiple markets quickly and efficiently.

Companies that produce hip, trendy products also do "evergreen" stories in VNR format. These are stories that are not tied to a particular event or date. That way, a news or informational TV show can drop in part or all of the video release at their leisure, without the pressure to ensure that the information is timely.

A satellite media tour is the release of live-broadcast information via satellite to multiple broadcast outlets. A tour must be scheduled approximately one week in advance. Remember that broadcasters have a limited amount of time in each program, so they need at least this much lead time to fit in a satellite tour.

It costs a minimum of several thousand dollars to do a satellite tour, capping out at about $25,000. But note that as technology gets better, this price is likely to fall substantially. Cities in or near most major markets will have satellite media groups listed in the yellow pages that can arrange one seamlessly.

For a satellite media tour to be effective, you need a notable public or corporate figure, because otherwise producers will not devote a segment of their broadcast time to airing it. The CEO of your firm (or inventor of your product) might count if he's compelling as a star in his own right, or if he's already out there in the press.

Trying to get someone of note to star in your video release is probably not a good idea. If there isn't a natural celebrity angle, forget it. For instance, in 2001, Kim Catrall (star of the mega TV show *Sex and the City*) did a satellite media tour to promote a new Nikon camera. She was so completely unnecessary to the news broadcasts that picked up the feed that the rest of the media lampooned the campaign. Nikon was laid out on the carpet for pursuing the media in this manner.

A satellite tour is best used to reach multiple markets at once. Most often, public companies use satellite tours to disseminate sensitive investor information quickly and in accordance with SEC regulations. The story you are promoting should be very newsworthy. Otherwise, few, if any, networks will pick up your feed.

A traditional press release should quickly follow the satellite broadcast to encourage the print media to carry the information as well. And in a new twist on sour grapes, send the same press release to those who didn't see the satellite tour to show them what they missed.

Wire Services

Wire services are news distribution outlets, such as Business Wire, PR Newswire, and the AP Wire, for corporate information. Journalists in search of potential stories visit them often.

The best way to use a wire is not to depend on it. They are helpful if you are a major company releasing information or if you are announcing a never-before-seen technology, but as with any other type of information, you'll find yourself lumped in with thousands of other announcements made every day.

That said, wire services are useful for establishing the history of a company. In other words, if you run a series of wire releases about your company, any reporter looking to find out more about you can turn a simple search into a chronological list of documented events and announcements.

To rise above the clutter, try attaching a photo to the release. Anything from a hardware device to a new-hire photo will help. We recommend Business Wire in most cases, because it carries the national business and Internet trade lists. E-mail your releases to newsroom@bizwire.com and indicate whom you are targeting—general reporters, business writers, and so on.

Getting a Handle on All of It

OKAY, AT THIS POINT in considering our soup-to-nuts listing of tactical approaches, you're exhausted, and you may not even know where to begin. We thought of that. To help you out, here's a timeline of what a typical media plan might look like. This sample plan could have all sorts of permutations, of course, but it will give you a basic framework and an idea of the work flow.

Ninety Days to All-Out Buzz

This is a proposed ninety-day (one annual quarter) plan for a customer relationship management product that is just launching.

The whole process starts with a kickoff meeting, where all parties will sit down and delve into every aspect of the business, competitive landscape, and industry positioning. Following that discussion, outline your business objectives and discuss these in depth with your executive management team. Get the necessary buy-ins and sign-offs before you begin, because it's important to give the overall strategy an opportunity to succeed, without being hamstrung by corporate politics.

The last process, tactical identification and development, incorporates most of the media strategies outlined below. Clearly, the dates and timing below are only suggestions.

Timeline:
Ninety Days to All-Out Buzz

A U G U S T

ACTIVITY	DATE
Creative session to identify core objectives	August 1
Research competitive landscape	Week of 8/1

Develop strategic PR plan based on core objectives	**Week of 8/1**
Identify key message points	**Week of 8/1**
Develop message tracks to follow first announcement	**Week of 8/1**
Devise story-pitching angles for target media	**Week of 8/8**
Conduct media training for potential company spokespersons	**Week of 8/8**
Create press kits (press releases, fact sheet, bios, corporate backgrounder, screen shots)	**Week of 8/8**
Develop comprehensive media target lists	**Week of 8/8**
Send biweekly progress report to relevant parties	**8/11 and 8/30**
Begin source filing principals with major publications	**Ongoing**
Pitch top-tier journalists on launch/ partnerships/clients	**Ongoing**
Proactive story pitching in new trends in product support	**Ongoing**
Research survey options for examining consumer attitudes toward customer service	**Week of 8/21**
Go out to the market with surveys— test out a few on colleagues to see if you get any results you think are noteworthy	**Week of 8/30**

SEPTEMBER

ACTIVITY	DATE
Meet to discuss company developments, upcoming announcements, new partnerships, etc.	Week of 9/4
Develop press release schedule	Week of 9/4
Develop media lists in vertical target markets in conjunction with new customers, partnerships, etc.	Week of 9/4
Identify key analysts	Week of 9/4
Arrange analyst tour	Week of 9/11
Conduct analyst tour	Week of 9/18
Pitch top-tier journalists on launch/ partnerships/clients	Ongoing
Proactive story pitching in new trends in product support	Ongoing
Survey development begins this week, time to finalize topic	Week of 9/18
Develop survey questions	Week of 9/25
Make changes and finalize survey	9/15, 9/31

OCTOBER

ACTIVITY	DATE
Meet to discuss company developments, upcoming announcements, new partnerships, etc.	Week of 10/2
Proactive pitching to vertical markets	Ongoing
Continue to pitch top-tier journalists on launch/partnerships/clients	Ongoing

Continue to refine and develop new pitch angles to track strategies	**Week of 10/9**
Obtain and analyze survey results	**Week of 10/9**
Develop case studies on current customers	**Week of 10/9**
Pitch case studies in trend pieces to top-tier target media	**Week of 10/9 and on**
Develop survey release strategy	**Week of 10/16**
Research and compile a list of recommended holiday media tours with gadget gurus	**Week of 10/16**
Release survey results	**Week of 10/23**
Conduct follow-up on survey announcement to media targets	**Ongoing**
Develop second-quarter PR plan	**Week of 10/23**
Analyze all the above and make changes to move forward immediately	**10/15, 10/31**

CHAPTER 4

Finding the Right News Hook

NOW THAT YOU HAVE AN IDEA of what good buzz can do for you, it's time to do your homework. It's a two-part assignment. First you need to figure out the competitors in your category and to see what type of press predecessors have received. If you study your competition wisely, you'll learn from the mistakes other people have made. Then you need to find a compelling reason to get media folks to take you seriously. That's your news hook. If you can suss out your competition effectively and then tap into a unique media hook, you are on your way to great press coverage.

Maybe that doesn't sound very glamorous, and you'd rather spend your time inventing ever-more-ingenious gimmicks to get press for yourself. There's something to be said for those looking to travel way beyond the fringe of the media, to explore new territory, and to boldly go where no entrepreneur has gone before—they simply better *also* be into doing their homework.

Let us explain. For every successful idea, there are thousands of clunkers. Most of those nonsensical wonders had some sort of a PR strategy, and in some cases, it was the best part of the business. With many Internet businesses, the glowing press coverage got to your door two seconds past a mouse click, but the profits always seemed to be quite late. The point: When you put your product in front of fickle, unforgiving, and intelligent consumers and journalists, you'd better get it right.

Take Good Notes

IN TERMS OF SUSSING OUT the competition, this is one area in which you need ideas on how to learn from what's been done before. You don't need to reinvent the wheel here; you only need to get good PR for your product. How did those successes you've noted unveil themselves, and what did they say and do to get their public to notice? Was a failure the result of using an approach that was too elitist? Did the company pay no mind to its competitor's message, or did it just forget to take the public's temperature and understand what it really wanted to hear? The case studies that follow elaborate on some PR successes and failures based on news hooks that work and those that miss their mark.

Sussing Out the Competition

In late 2001, a weakening economy and a nationwide terrorist scare that was felt across America kept the skies quiet and travel-free. The fleets of the mightiest airlines embarked with their cabins only one-third full. In many cases, the lack of passengers kept them from even making it to the tarmac. Employees at American, Delta, and British Airways were given their walking papers by the thousands, and even some of the most stable international carriers, such as Swiss Air, just closed up shop without warning.

Amidst all of this airline industry chaos, there was JetBlue, the U.S.-based, start-up airline company that found profitability in a period of total disaster. How was a newcomer able to flourish while other battle-tested carriers faltered? They took notes. The airline industry was so set in its ways that it was unwilling to make changes, fearing risk and reduced profits. JetBlue was one of the few carriers—Southwest, Delta Express, and Sun Jet were some of the others—to suss out the situation. JetBlue observed how the competition behaved in the pinch and learned what to do differently and so much better.

The world was watching what the transport behemoths would do, but in fact, they did very little. Passengers wouldn't board a plane for fear of hijackers, and those who did demanded a few security measures, such as impenetrable pilot cockpits and a flight crew trained in self-defense. As Katie Couric and every other morning, noon, and evening anchor talked about bulletproof security cabin doors, airliners bucked the suggestion, claiming the extra weight would require more fuel (read: more money), and all of this would shave away at the profitability of putting one of their big birds on the runway.

During the debate, JetBlue was calmly rolling its brand-new planes into hangars, preparing them for the company's big story. JetBlue executives ushered columnists and camera crews onto one of their airbuses to demonstrate the first bulletproof and impenetrable cabin door, guaranteeing the captain and crew stay at the helm while in flight, no matter what. JetBlue said that it planned to absorb the cost of extra fuel itself, without raising the price of admission for its happy passengers. It claimed that this was the least it could do to ensure safety and a feeling that real security alterations were already happening.

What impressions did the media take away from that press conference? Added security with no muss, no fuss. By watching their strangely slow competitors, JetBlue learned exactly what not to do, and although it might have cost the company a few extra gallons per flight, its planes continue to leave the runways with cabins full of passengers a little more at ease and ready to fly.

New Tricks for Old Dogs

Watching the competition doesn't mean only finding out what others have done wrong. In fact, the best ideas are usually advancements of what others have already accomplished. Just as Alexander Graham Bell found fame with an invention that perhaps wasn't entirely his (Antonio Meucci's clan is still waiting for patent infringement checks on his invention), you, too, can achieve success by learning what those before you have done well. Consider the following.

If you don't live near a good pizzeria, you probably put up with pizza from a chain pizzeria, or worse, from a frosty box in the grocery store freezer section. However unpleasant a meal it might be, there's big, big money in those freezers and a lot of business at stake. PR gimmickry in the food industry goes a long way, and no one wants, or can afford, to be the outfit pushing the ho-hum meal when their competitor three inches away is offering something new. But pizza's pretty standard, right? Not necessarily.

In pursuit of that "thing" that drives buzz and gets soccer moms buying their pies for a hungry team, DiGiorno's PR and marketing guys put their heads together and figured out what would turn their tired pizza into something new and fun—rising dough, bringing it one step closer to the real thing. Now DiGiorno's had something to talk about, something that was different than what you would expect from a regular pizza. Its "chefs" hit the morning TV talk show circuit, pushing the puffy pizza for parties, dinner, and late-night snacks. Journalists across the country were given wind of the new idea and a whiff of the new and improved pies. It only took a simple difference, but it was enough to take an ordinary, everyday product and turn it into something new for the media.

What You See Is What You Get Out of It

This phrase explains basic PR: What the public sees is what it gets out of the message. For instance, there are currently hundreds of financial institutions gunning for your checking account. Some of them are after the multimillionaires, some target new families, and others, like Citigroup and E*TRADE, prefer the emerging rich. Both of these companies are in a PR war to attract the same group of customers, those with $100,000 or more to invest and the desire to actively manage their financial accounts.

Citigroup finds itself forced to innovate in the battle with, of all things, relative upstart E*TRADE. Since its roots are in traditional banking—tellers, early hours, and advisers behind oak desks—Citigroup has needed to publicize its ability to operate twenty-four hours a day online, compete in the trading game, and give its customers the ability to manage their funds on the Web.

On the other hand, E*TRADE, the hotshot, home day-trading company, needed to acquire a bit of wing-tip culture once the economy slowed and any stock worth trading evaporated. To compete day in and day out, E*TRADE maintained its humorous, edgy appeal through advertising. However, it also used the media to hype its other worthwhile products, such as brand-new, physical financial centers throughout the country and sensible mortgage offerings.

E*TRADE and Citigroup continually monitor what each other is doing, to determine which messages are out there in the media and to figure out what they can tell customers to make them devoted clients. In the end, it's up to the consumer to decide what's best, but it's up to the PR professionals to be aggressive in noting what the real differences are.

What They Aren't Doing

While you're taking notes, don't just look at what your competition is doing. Take note of what they *aren't* doing, too. *GQ, Details, Esquire,* and *Gear* were going after (and continue to target) the same Kia-driving, young, male demographic. But features on $1,500 suits, ski trips to Aspen, and 500-horsepower boy toys weren't clicking with the fresh-out-of-the-frat-house set. Instead, all of these publications appealed to the forty-something group, but not just any forty-somethings: the type who have cufflinks and know all the techniques for slowing down the progression of time on their faces.

On the other side of the Atlantic, Felix Dennis, the British uber-publisher, watched these American magazines battle for the wrong demographic and planned his attack on the group of sophisticates the others were missing. Dennis knew how to win them over. He needed to give the media what would make the magazine front-page material with this crowd, the thing that no other men's mag was dishing out: breasts. Product-wise, Dennis's *Maxim* magazine, bursting with scantily clad women, was passed off as under-achieving porn by the publishing industry, but in two short years he had the last laugh. The cover of *Maxim* wound up gracing the pages of dozens of other magazines that reported the exploits of his sexy periodical. Soon the buzz on E! and in the papers was that for young, red-blooded men, *Maxim* was the magazine to buy.

The media lauded *Maxim* for its cutting content, tongue-in-cheek humor, sex goddesses, and massive circulation. Like David Letterman in Leno's shadow, *Details* and *GQ* have yet to recover from the introduction of *Maxim* and most likely will not for a long time to come.

Look in the Couch Cushions

ONCE YOU'VE SPENT some time checking out *your* competition, take a hard look at your organization. What would make a great story for the media? Start by looking in the couch cushions of your business, because good stories sometimes hide in unlikely places. Think not only of the things that make your organization most proud of your business or product, but also maybe the feat you can't believe you've actually pulled off. Most likely, there's something challenging going on inside your organization that can be made into news, if you package it properly.

Quite possibly, that good story can come from what you would ordinarily consider your worst news. The media will always be more attracted to a story with a clear and obvious problem and how it was overcome. If you have such a setback, try to find the silver lining and make news with it.

Here's an example of how you can spin a strategic misstep into a news hook, thus turning lemons into lemonade, so to speak. Draw The Line was a relatively new branding company in the late '90s that discovered it had the same name as another, similar company. Not surprisingly, Draw The Line had a really tough time branding itself. The company needed to change its name, but without bringing attention to the problem and without losing any customers or revenue.

So what did Draw The Line do? The company went beyond merely filing for a name change and made that change newsworthy. Its first task was to become Underline (with what we dubbed "control U," the underline key in Microsoft Word, as their trademark) and then to take its new message to the press. During a period that saw a spurt of great entrepreneurial zeal, the media loved the story that two companies had popped up with the same name, and so the marketing press began to follow Underline's mission to control its own brand identity.

The Feeding Frenzy

The news media look too hard at what the news "could be," often harder than at what the news "is." For those of us practicing PR, that's a plus like you wouldn't believe, because when the news is slow you can have a field day by creating opportunities for reporters in need. (They might not ever admit this happens, but please ....)

Here's a case in point. The summer of 2001 was the summer of the shark. Statistically, there were fewer attacks nationwide than there had been in previous years, but seemingly weekly episodes of underwater ravaging captured America's fears as well as the head-lines. So how did a relatively undeserving great white shark get on the cover of Time?

It was a combination of circumstances. One of the biggest angles the great white had going for him was that he was newsworthy by asso-ciation. For the past three years or so, Floridians had been getting more and more up in arms about the tourist-aimed cottage industry of shark feeding boats, dumping chum and other shark delicacies

David and Goliath

Another common situation from which you can craft a news hook is the challenge to compete effectively against larger companies with much deeper pockets. For example, BigStar Entertainment, which hawks online videos and DVDs with plans eventually to sell downloadable entertainment, wanted to position itself in the press as an accessible alternative to stores like Blockbuster. This publicly traded e-commerce company was the first to market video movies, but later had to compete with the online divisions of established brick-and-mortar stores, such as Blockbuster Enter-tainment. BigStar's market was easy to explain to the press. How-ever, from the online movie-store angle, the challenge lay in dif-ferentiating BigStar from the bazillions of other dot-com movie retailers and other kinds of online retailers in general.

closer and closer to the water of Boca Raton homes. The same thing had been going on in California, too. This was a steaming-hot local issue.

The coastal media associated the attacks with the feeding debate and gave a usually lightly covered story a ton of airtime and ink. Quite possibly, they surmised, it was a pure coincidence worth reporting. In the TV news biz, if it bleeds, it leads.

The unprecedented number of "shock attacks," as the Bostonians call them, didn't propel this story into the global news. Hardly. Those underfed sharks have been steadily decreasing in past years, and, as noted, there were no more attacks than usual in August 2001, some weeks or days away from the biggest news story of the new century. The reason the story was even reported nationwide had to do with the so-called Silly Season when media just can't find a thing to cover.

All of this simply goes to show that what we consider news is highly subjective. Therefore, when the "news" is slow, rejoice, because it might be the best chance you ever get to crank up your buzz machine.

To stand out, the company needed to promote its conservative but effective marketing strategy, as well as its management's many years of experience with the Internet, direct marketing, and entertainment industry. The other idea was to fit BigStar into current trend stories that related to its strengths in content, direct marketing, and, in a unique twist, on company culture.

How did BigStar do that? First, it carefully limited press-release distribution to one per week to heighten the impact of each story. Also, the company released only the news that would be relevant to reporters, such as "BigStar is in talks with X to create a new way to select favorite videos online" or "BigStar releases its third ad campaign of the year." For news on promotions or consumer angles, targeted pitches to vertical markets and goody bags for key reporters fit the bill. The Academy Awards ceremony, for instance, made for a nice news hook and a "peg" for all entertainment-oriented journalists.

The year 2000 was the year when the Oscars (the statuettes themselves) had gone missing, as the saying goes. Ultimately, they turned up in a West Hollywood dumping ground. To play up the comical angle of all this, BigStar commissioned chocolate statuettes that looked like Oscars, put them in tiny garbage can-like creations, and messengered them to reporters. (A few got lost, of course, making it an even funnier story.)

Another approach played off the rent-versus-buy angle for videos and DVDs: Why rent when, for a few dollars more, you can own a movie forever? Tongue firmly in cheek, the company placed an ad in Times Square in New York that said, "Stop paying rent. www.bigstar.com!" It also parked a VW Beetle with the same slogan outside a major Blockbuster's store and watched with glee (from a publicity perspective) as the employees called the police. Don't try this at home, folks—we're not suggesting you dream up stunts that could put you on the wrong side of the law. The point here is that the outlandishness of this act drew a lot of attention to BigStar.

The company also got a lot of attention for its IPO, for some unusual reasons that turned into a terrific news hook. Blockbuster missed a deadline to go public. By contrast, BigStar finished its IPO right on schedule. It used this David/Goliath angle to great advantage in the press.

The Story of the Season

In order to spotlight your company effectively, it's important to grasp what is getting the media's attention right now. What is it that you're actually looking for? The most important part of this story is the seasonal aspect, something so big that it gets everyone's attention.

At this very moment, in your local paper and buzzing through the atmosphere, bouncing off satellite dishes and wending its way through parties, is "the big story": the thing the country can't get enough of. It might have nothing to do with your business, idea, or service, but you can always find a way to hook into the big buzz. Whether it's a "cultural phenomenon" or merely something *everyone's* chatting on about, a little bit of creative meditating, and you can hook in.

The story of the season is a term for a breathing, growing, living thing. It's feeding off the public, and the masses are feeding off it, encouraging it to grow, poking it for more of what it's got. And it gets bigger and stronger with every inquiry. Like a virus in a petri dish, the season's big story comes about only with careful cultivation and can only exist under certain conditions. The story of the season is thriving because it's found a way to tap into the national sentiment.

Let's take Michael Jackson, for instance. After six years, in 2002 he came out of hiding to put out another album. Although many fans considered it a disappointment and the *real* music critics panned it, celebrities from every genre ran to support Michael's tour, and he dominated the mainstream press once again.

Why? On the pop music scene, "pop synth" bands such as New Order, Depeche Mode, and even Missy Elliott had taken over the airwaves in recent years. Boy bands were sparring in Virgin Mega Stores, and Britney and Christina were dueling on soda cans. America was scoffing at these young entertainers and starting to question when pop would be kaput. Just then, Michael re-entered the picture. The country was sure that he would refuel the America's pop-music tanks, and the concerts sold out in minutes. There was nothing new or fresh in the music, but it was perfect timing for the national mood and nostalgia.

It wasn't that Michael's album was good; it was more that at the time, America's obsession with pop stars was at a fifty-two–week high, giving MJ easy entry into the market. The same goes for industries outside of entertainment. Every week there's a news bit that wins the lion's share of airtime and print space. If you, your business or product has anything to do with what the media is talking about, you have to capitalize on the buzz and grab on. The press will be more likely to listen to your story, and you'll get the coverage.

If It's Newsy and You Know It, Clap Your Hands

Got it? A news hook is the most compelling part of your story. You probably know that by now, but what you need to realize is that the hook doesn't have to be real news. That doesn't mean you should go out there with a non-news item; it means that you should be creative and *make* the news, as BigStar did in the examples given above. The bottom line: If it's *newsy,* use it. And on top of that, an important thing to remember is that what you find the most compelling part of your story may be miles apart from the aspect that the media and opinion leaders are most interested in.

Take the idea of using holiday or seasonal tie-ins, for example. It may sound hackneyed, but there's still plenty of life left in that angle if you can find a fresh way to tweak it, and this is particularly important for retailers and manufacturers that depend on a seasonal shot in the arm, revenue-wise. Consider eCandy, an online candy store for consumers, with products ranging from supermarket sweets to hard-to-find European chocolates. After launching in mid-January 2000, eCandy wanted to raise awareness among general consumers in an effort to drive traffic to the site before the all-important Easter and Mother's Day holidays.

The challenge eCandy faced was competing with the hundreds of other online and brick-and-mortar companies targeting consumers for the same holidays. At the same time, the company was not ready to announce any new confectionery products or high-profile company developments. To raise eCandy above the holiday noise, and to garner quick results on the tail end of the seasonal Easter stories *before* the rapidly approaching Mother's Day, the company decided to capitalize on the heavy media attention given to last-minute taxpayers on April 15.

The company's slogan for this angle was "eCandy Gives Sweet Returns On-Line." To play that up, it hired a man on stilts dressed as Uncle Sam to pass out eCandy chocolate coins to reward all the last-minute taxpayers at New York's and Los Angeles's main post offices. To create additional hype for this event, eCandy sent out chocolate press releases requesting that reporters click on a special URL informing them about eCandy's Tax Day promotion with Uncle Sam. This specialized (and easy to pull off) tax-day event resulted in tremendous broadcast and print coverage (including Associated Press, the *New York Daily News,* several television channels, and trade magazines) that carried the eCandy name to more than 6.5 million candy consumers, with the eCandy slogan mentioned almost every time. The tremendous spike in brand recognition and Web surfer curiosity drove site traffic, and ultimately sales, through the roof.

Freshen Up

All products can do with a news hook that makes people see them as brand-spanking new or, at the very least, a twist on an existing theme. This is particularly true for magazines and any sort of publication. Allow this unorthodox example: *City Family* was developed as a magazine geared to the needs of new immigrants to New York. At first, the news media refused to take it seriously. As one academic told National Public Radio the day *City Family* launched: "I don't see how this can help. They can't eat the darn thing!"

City Family magazine came about because its publisher, Arthur Schiff, was an early proponent of the food stamp program in New York. He knew that immigrants and "new New Yorkers" did not have a magazine meant for them—a publication that would address their problems, questions, and desires. Coming from a political background and knowing this group well, he started it himself, in English and Spanish. The immediate reaction was

CEOs and the Word

Gosh that's a big desk! And are all these secretaries yours? It's nice to be on top, buddy, but just because you're running the show and (almost) everyone's answering to you, it doesn't mean you've gotten the art of PR down.

There are a few things to remember when it comes to managing a CEO who's a press hog. The thing about CEOs is they all have friends in high places and continually meet reporters at one cocktail party or another. They think they can do it all themselves. Not only that, they think journalists are there to do them a "favor"—that's the "F" word in this book.

Truth is, journalists who chat them up aren't their friends at all. They cover the beat, and they're waiting for any less-than-intelligent statement to fall from your boss's loose lips.

It pays to force the issue before this happens: Make sure your CEO understands the needed boundaries when it comes to talking to the press.

laughter. People (among them, purported urban "experts") said, "Why bother? A magazine for the poorer population—who would advertise in it?" Especially since it was free.

City Family acted fast and furiously by sending out copies of the magazine and material to hundreds of immigrant, entrepreneur, city, and novelty features writers. (Novelty features writers are those dozen reporters in your hometown or city who write about whatever they fancy. You have to find angles that make them say "ah.")

These were the first to see what a unique tale Schiff's was. Once he learned how to deliver a consistent message to the press (see Chapter 6, "It's YOUR Interview!"), he started to streamline responses so that people would see the good *City Family* was doing. Soon the magazine had a circulation of 250,000 and was a

Then there's messaging. We've told you that the best stories always have a challenge in them. CEOs don't ever like to say the company is struggling or performing less than phenomenally, so they fill interview time with windy messages ripped from the marketing material. Many love to send sleep-inducing PowerPoints to F-owing reporter pals. It's all very salesy.

Hard as it may be, you must step in and set it right. You need to tell reporters the facts, ma'am, and you must create a CEO who can talk the straight poop. If you don't, it all falls apart. The story won't happen, the journalist covering your beat will have an eternal beef with you, not with your CEO, and you'll never get in that pub again. It's your gig; don't let 'em push you around.

And who will be the angriest? The CEO! Those at the top are often tough to handle when it comes to egos. But if you're the professional getting exposure for the firm, you were placed at your desk, albeit smaller, for a reason. It's time for you to prove your place elegantly and powerfully.

huge hit in the media circles. The first major story hit the *Daily News's* City section, followed by the all-essential vertical advertiser and alternative weeklies (*Adweek, Advertising Age, Village Voice, Baltimore City Paper,* and *West Side Spirit* in Manhattan) and pieces in *Crain's, Newsweek,* and national magazine media, such as *Folio,* the magazine for the magazine publishing industry.

Then, after a year in business, *City Family* was named one of the top start-ups of the prior twelve months by the *Library Journal* ... and after that it was a short trip to the big leagues, press-wise: the *Wall Street Journal* and the *Los Angeles Times*—and then, a year later, the *New York Times. City Family* magazine subsequently expanded into four cities along with an international edition, as well as an online edition.

Beware the Cult of Personality

It was Arthur Schiff's vision of how *City Family* could serve the immigrant population's needs, combined with his ability to personify that vision, that elevated the magazine to the national radar screen. Often that's exactly what small companies have going for them in the way of news hooks: a visionary (and sometimes plain quirky) entrepreneur at the helm. But for companies like these, the cult of personality is a double-edged sword.

How's that, you say? Cult of *what*? That's what happens to a company when its press revolves solely around its CEO or other top management, rather than the company's real news hooks.

Our favorite cult-of-personality-gone-wrong story features Joseph Park of aforementioned Kozmo.com, a failed firm whose mission was to receive Internet orders and to deliver goods throughout New York City. One of the many Web start-ups to emerge out of New York's digital cornucopia, it started off by deploying a handful of bike messengers onto the streets to deliver movies, books, CDs, magazines, food, electronics, and more—from the Internet to your door in less than an hour.

Like any company in its infancy, Kozmo knew it was mission-critical to catch the eye of potential consumers and investors alike. To fuel expansion and ensure survival, this unique organization needed to be taken seriously in the business press, not viewed as gimmicky.

The company launched a media campaign to position itself as something more than a local video store on the Web. Rather, it wanted to be seen as an innovative company poised to revolutionize the way corporations and consumers use the Web. At a 1999 luncheon to introduce the emerging industry of pervasive computing, Kozmo.com seized the day. When Kozmo's Joseph Park started his presentation by asking the attendees their favorite type of ice cream, people seemed confused, but as he spoke, Big Joe punched in the order, and before he'd finished his address, a crowd of skeptics was transformed into a throng of ice cream-eating believers as Kozmo messengers delivered their favorites quickly and accurately.

The company capitalized on the momentum created at the event and didn't let up. It basked in the accolades of *Forbes, Red Herring, Newsweek, BusinessWeek, Kiplinger's, Vanity Fair, The New Yorker, The Economist, Financial Times,* among others. *New York* magazine featured Joseph Park in its "New Yorkers of 1999" cover story, and *Silicon Alley Reporter* labeled him among the "Top CEOs of 1999."

Six bicycles and a lot of determination grew to more than 1,000 pairs of wheels, delivering everything from the latest video releases to high-end electronics. Investors identified Kozmo.com as a sure bet, and consumers flocked to the site with a cultish zeal.

But where are Park and Kozmo now? After a three-year run, Kozmo ceased operations in 2001. In the end, the company learned that you can't just rest on the repute of one person; the deals put together have to earn you cash in addition to headlines. That might sound obvious, but plenty of entrepreneurs get carried away with their early successes (and even their later ones). Ego is a by-product of intense press, but you can't let it be your end game. Amen.

Testing Your Wings

Let's move on to another example. What do you do when you're a struggling new company looking to attract investors? Lewis Schiff, an entrepreneur who founded ArmchairMillionaire.com, coauthored *The Armchair Millionaire* (Pocket Star, 2001), and launched *Worth* Online, knew a good business model when he saw one. Investorama was the most complete directory of investing sites on the Web, with more than 11,000 links in 141 categories. With Schiff's investment, it was poised to become one of the biggest personal finance affinity directories on the Web, but he needed an additional investment from a smart angel investor or venture capitalist. The question was how to rise above the clamor and convince investors that the enterprise was worth taking a closer look at.

The answer was to make Lewis Schiff a fixture in Silicon Valley for twenty days. He stated his wishes loud and clear—on a 14'x48' billboard on Highway 101! Schiff's billboard debuted on April 15. The idea was a bold and brash one and drew attention not only to Lewis's sassy New York roots, but also to his imagination for and confidence in the company. The choice of Highway 101 was an easy one: As a major highway running right through Silicon Valley, it's the road most traveled by the type of person whom Lewis was trying to reach.

What happened was fun and not a little controversial. Controversy—unless it gets you thrown in jail—can be good for your press book. And how. The big Web portal Yahoo! was angry with Schiff for having the audacity to say on his billboard, "Help us become the Yahoo! of financial advice." Well, after nineteen days, Schiff promised to take down the billboard after the Yahoo! lawyers got a little uppity. Schiff told his story to the press, neatly leaving out the fact that he'd planned to take the billboard down on the twentieth day anyway. The now-infamous billboard appeared on the front page of the *New York Times* and in the *Wall Street Journal, San Francisco Chronicle,* and *San Jose Mercury News,* not to mention in numerous broadcasts, too. Schiff's arousing the ire of Yahoo! and his larger-than-life mug looming over 101 was too much fun for the media to pass up. Not only did several investors come through, but another story came out about his success.

Here's another idea for a news hook: How about handing some fun to generally bored business reporters? That's another great route to success. The British-born "More Balls Than Most" (we kid you not) was a very successful game maker looking to expand its market in the early 1990s. The company created stress-relieving juggling balls for high-level, high-anxiety-prone executives. These were sold everywhere from Harrod's in the United Kingdom to Macy's and Saks here in the United States.

MBTM also wanted badly to make juggling *huge* in the

United States. More than that, it had the unorthodox notion of bringing it to America's businesses as a way to reduce stress. But in 1993, juggling was hardly a trend in the United States. It was perceived as a difficult and specialized skill that was frivolous and, well, silly. Why would anyone take the time, especially in a corporate setting?

MBTM positioned itself as a company ("those funny, smart Brits") that sells skills. As a consumer product, the firm offered an unusual, high-quality gift that increased confidence and aided relaxation. In the corporate sector, it portrayed juggling as an invaluable way to instill self-esteem and risk-taking abilities—two qualities that corporations want in their executives. Juggling is also an excellent metaphor for multi-task management—juggling priorities, if you will.

MBTM's profile and profits rose steadily since its arrival in this country. The number of corporate jugglers was five times greater than predicted, and that's because of positive press coverage. But to attract the press's attention, the techniques had to be as unorthodox as the company. For example, in an interview on a public radio program, the company chairman taught the host to juggle transatlantically over the phone. In another event, MBTM staff presented themselves as juggling madmen, and after they held juggling fests on public streets, with corporate types leading the fray, they were on their way.

MBTM probably got the most attention, however, by simply showing people what it does. The company created opportunities for journalists to come to juggling sessions in executive boardrooms in every major city, where they could finally see CEOs learn how to juggle for real.

Never Mind the Dust Bunnies

You might be thinking that it's easy enough to come up with creative angles when you have an offbeat product (although it isn't always easy). But what happens when your product is a little less glamorous, perhaps even a bit dusty around the edges? The paper company Arjo Wiggins had no news to speak of, and its product, Polyart, was no longer the new kid on the block. Polyart is an environmentally friendly, waterproof, tear-resistant, nontoxic polyethylene paper. The company had been manufacturing it for almost eleven years, but had never done any sort of media relations.

Arjo Wiggins decided it was time to raise Polyart's profile during the year of the first Earth Day. It would be a big day for ecology, but Arjo Wiggins's sales were down, and the company wanted to generate some interest in its products. Operating under the "don't ask, don't tell" philosophy, the company ignored the age factor and targeted new product reporters at paper, label, graphic arts, and environmental publications. These reporters received a letter designed to make them sit up and take notice. The release was printed on a tough sheet of Polyart, and reporters were dared to rip the release in half, spill coffee on it, and even burn it. That was the news: "You've never seen this before, and now you must—must—try it."

Reporters ate it up. And since it was the first time any of them *had* seen or heard of it, they naturally assumed it was fresh from the lab. During the course of a few months, hundreds of mentions in a variety of publications popped up, and Arjo Wiggins USA was flooded with phone calls from all over the globe. The state of Israel decided to use Polyart for its new driver's licenses, while Greenpeace saw its value for event tickets. Ultimately, the company had to hire extra employees just to handle the new flood of inquiries. That's a challenge most companies seem to enjoy.

Fixin' To Stick Around

Let's take the opposite tack. Suppose your idea is a bit ahead of its time. Now that the dot-com bubble has burst and the overall economic mood is more sober, you need to convince the media that two years from now, your idea will be not a fad but a fixture. You want to convey the notion that your Next Big Thing is big enough to stick around.

The NBT is something you have to believe in. That's hard to do. So many people claim that what they're bringing to the table is the NBT, and unfortunately, they prove to be wrong most of the time. That doesn't mean you can't generate some positive press in the meantime, however. In 1996, before the dot-com boom, FieldWorks, a company in Eden Prairie, Minnesota, was manufacturing rugged laptop computers, built to withstand just about anything. With nothing more than a few clips from trade publications, how could this company get reporters to sit up and take notice, when big-gun Panasonic was threatening to produce this type of machine itself? (In fact, Panasonic never did.) How could they prove they were the next big thing?

In order to prove the company's NBT status, it was necessary to look no further than their customer list, which was mind-blowing: NASA; MIR; U.S. Army, Navy, and Air Force; Disney; AT&T; the New York Police Department; and others of similar stature. The strategy was clear: Name-drop left and right. If that didn't excite reporters enough, the company invited them to throw one of the FieldWorks computers across the room, run a car over it, submerge it in ice, and stand on it and jump!

That did it. FieldWorks generated a considerable buzz, and *Fortune, PC Computing, Wired,* CNN, NBC, and dozens of others quickly ran glowing previews of the new FieldWorks machines. It also didn't hurt that a FieldWorks computer turned on immediately, without any booting time. At that time, this was *the* big complaint of corporate consumer users. To highlight this aspect, the company posed this thought-provoking question to the press: "Would you wait two full minutes for your car to start?"

The media attention FieldWorks gained helped this tiny company grow and make a name. Their plant doubled in size in just a year, and before they were sold two years later to a huge local conglomerate, they struggled to keep up with the pace of customer inquiries.

Where Angels Fear to Tread

FieldWorks was a company firmly identified as devising a good and useful twist on an important product. But how do you handle media coverage if your product has a potential for consumer and media backlash? This can sometimes happen when a product is controversial or not quite all it's made out to be. These are delicate situations, and you need to give a lot of thought to what the potential traps and criticisms are likely to be, and to play up your product's strongest features to offset any impediments to market acceptance. For example, a website that teaches college students how to use credit cards responsibly (while selling them credit cards, of course) wanted to increase traffic to its website. The challenge was to position it as a valuable financial tool despite the fact that the site offers credit cards to students.

To that end, and to increase serious, college-age awareness of StudentCredit.com, the site held a "Debt Pay Off" promotion. The contest paid off the debts of ten college students and gave them the opportunity to start fresh at managing their credit cards, using the advice the site served up. In addition, the news hook focused on the site's positive features, such as its free bill reminder service and its "ten steps to good credit," while positioning the company's CEO as a financial expert for college students.

In a few months, people stopped doubting the agenda of the owners, and in fact, stories about them appeared in the *New York Post* and in college newspapers everywhere. The chief of the company, a hard-edged businessman during the week and a young surfer dude on the weekends, was featured in *Brand Week,* the *Boston Herald, Money,* and the *Oregonian* and the *Tower Light* (two large-circulation, alternative weeklies). He also spoke on live radio in college towns everywhere. Somehow, the potential conflict never made the light of day, and the site has continued to grow from its exposure, reaching thousands of new students every year.

Along similar lines, how do you manage a news hook when you have news that no one in the company wants you to talk about yet, but you are, unfortunately, in the throes of a controversy you didn't even start? Sesame Workshop, formerly known as the Children's Television Workshop, is the venerable educational organization that created and produces the TV show *Sesame Street.* In 1996, Congress was working hard and fast to create privacy rules so that shows like *Sesame* would not take advantage of the younger set on the newish medium called the Internet.

At the time, Tina Sharkey was the president of the CTW interactive division, and she found herself thrust into a difficult position. As manager of the first-ever website for the Children's Television Workshop (CTW.org), she had been handed a challenging mission. After all, CTW was famous for *Sesame Street,* but it didn't have a publishing firm, a cable station, or even its own toy line (these businesses were all farmed out). This "Internet thing" was the thirty-year-old company's way to make it into the big time as a media conglomerate!

But the site wouldn't be ready for quite some time. Sharkey was told that launching in the fall was fine, but she was not permitted to discuss the content with the press. So the only thing CTW could do to publicize its new website, without attaching specifics to it, was to get the word out quickly about the network's philosophy on website content for children. The company did get press coverage in a number of business and Internet publications, as well as daily newspapers.

The bad news: The privacy situation was heating up in Congress, and regulations for advertising or marketing via e-mail to kids was about to be turned into a bill. So instead of waiting for the results of the legislation, the CEO used Congress's interest as a news hook and met with several Washington lobbyists to present the CTW "stance" to the media.

In this way, CTW became a leader in the Internet privacy arena, rather than a follower. And the best part was that CTW was among the first to remind Congress that some privacy rules were simply not doable. For example, asking a child to fax a signed-by-Mom permission letter to an online company negates the whole point of the Internet. (That rule was, mercifully, shot down.)

This excellent media coverage was due, in great part, to the fact that CTW spoke up and to the fact that it had established its credibility early by laying some good PR groundwork. Today, CTW has become a force to be reckoned with in the online world, side by side with bigger networks like Nickelodeon's Nick.com and granddaddy Walt himself, Disney.com.

Grills Just Wanna Have Fun

Up to now everything we've told you in this chapter revolves around being inventive with your news hooks. But the fact is that sometimes there just isn't much news, or at least none that you want to talk about. That doesn't mean you can't invent some of your own (but no fibbing, now). Let us explain. Back in the summer of 2001, with e-commerce in question and the market at an all-time low, bad feelings about our economy were all around us. Amazon.com wanted to create some positive news to deflect attention away from The Street and to prove that its CEO, Jeff Bezos, is indeed a visionary with a sense of humor.

At the same time, Amazon also wanted to shed a little light on its "Honor System," a program that helps smaller sites collect money from users. We came up with the idea of a barbecue, hosted by Honor System devotees and comic geniuses from Modern Humorist (www.modernhumorist.com), that featured the grilling skills of Bezos himself. Counter to what the PR handbook preaches, the summer, especially July, is the perfect time to grab media attention with such events. Expecting many to consider the barbecue a hoax or a prank, we got the buzz swirling about the barbecue a week beforehand with an item in *USA Today*. The barbecue was also mentioned in the *New York Observer's* weekly guide, the AP Daybook, and the *New York Times*.

A good event needs to be a bit exclusive. The best and brightest financial, business, and cultural journalists were invited to the Bezos barbeque, and they all jumped at the opportunity. Syndicated network crews were among the attendees, ensuring that the coverage continued to spread well beyond New York (and the United States).

The barbecue was one of the most successful events Amazon.com had ever pulled off. More than 100 journalists attended from *US News & World Report, Time, Newsweek, Business-Week,* the *Wall Street Journal, Red Herring, Money, Fortune, Forbes,* MSNBC, CNN, Bloomberg TV, Associated Press, Reuters, and other publications. The barbecue, which was the first announcement-free press event in Amazon.com's history, encouraged scores of left-of-center, feel-good articles.

In an article in media-relations trade magazine *PR Week,* a reporter noted: "The week following the barbecue, Amazon.com posted its quarterly earnings and conceded that the positive media hype around the event improved the atmosphere for its announcement."

Chest Out, Shoulders High

On to the *meat*-ia of PR. Now that you've learned how to identify your competition and polish your news hook, the next steps are learning how to pitch your story to the media and becoming the confident spokesperson you must be to win over the press. Over and over again, we find that the major impediment to aggressive and effective PR is fear, even on the part of very accomplished people. But there's nothing magical about dealing with the press: If you bring something of value to the media, with verve, gusto, and glamorous passion, they eat it up. It's simple. Get out of here. Read Chapter 5.

Winding Up for the Pitch

PITCHING YOUR STORY. Just saying those three little words makes people shake a little. People new to the media are frequently surprised to hear that most feature, trend, or personality stories, not to mention business stories, find their way into the media because somebody picked up the phone. If it wasn't you, your name isn't in today's paper.

Pitching stories to reporters and convincing them to pay attention is something that public relations professionals do on a regular basis. It's a skill that you can acquire with some practice, but to be successful at it you must stick to some very orthodox, and quite specific, principles, namely:

❑ Do your homework.

❑ Be able to answer questions and know how to send more information when it's needed, but in a way that won't distract a reporter.

❑ Do it all in twenty seconds.

In Manhattan, the streets are swarming with salespeople. They comb the streets, rising and falling in skyscraper elevators, selling everything from T1 connector cables and long-distance phone service to air conditioners, photocopiers, and the ever-popular paper shredders! Sadly for them, most offices dash all their dreams of riches with signs like "Solicitors Not Welcome," often accompanied by the yikes-producing "Will Be Prosecuted for Loitering."

In our office, the sign's different. It simply reads, "Mean Solicitors Will Be Chastised." We don't take kindly to anyone with a grudge, but if you're pitching, we'll hear you out. It's what we call pitch karma: You pitch, we listen; we pitch, you listen.

As we see it, salesman-bashing is hypocritical. Virtually every company and economic system, for that matter, is based on transactions of goods and services and the hard work of salespeople. We're all salesmen, every one of us. We all just may not have the guts to do it door to door.

Public relations is sales in its purest form, so if you want to be successful, suck it up and consider the evening caller your brother. You're on the phone to sell ideas, sell facts, and sell the story of your product and company. But before you pick up the phone, lay out your call sheet, or think of what you're going to say; you have to get into sales mode. Real success lies in finding that state of ultimate confidence where it's impossible for someone to say no to you. It's a bit of brazenness, and it's inside every successful salesperson. We just have to figure out what summons it.

We'll let you in on a personal secret: Once a month, members of our firm watch all or any combination of *Glengarry Glen Ross, Wall Street,* and *Boiler Room.* Those three movies are the lynchpin to "pitchin' pitching" success because they're gritty, edgy, and oozing with self-absorbed confidence, the kind you may need to sell your story ten times a day. The lines in those films—such as, "What's my name? I drove here in an $80,000 BMW; that's my name!"—can keep us fueled for days of pitching.

The importance of confidence and swagger can't be stressed enough. Journalists (at times) are like hungry dogs, waiting to pick off a plump little PR person as if he were a pork chop. For example, a CNBC reporter recently said to an RLM associate who was trying to pitch a story, "Didn't you read that article that talks about the job market being so bad that even Harvard grads are going to work for you PR folks?" The reporter was trying to denigrate and derail her. Without missing a beat, she responded, "Didn't hear that. But it sounds interesting. So, let's talk about this story."

Resilience and self-assurance will give your listener pause and you the power to pitch. Spend some time and determine what it takes to get you into *your* zone. For example, a pitch-a-holic pal of ours can only pitch while standing. It keeps him alert and amped; otherwise he lapses back into his everyday, unbrazen self.

Okay, now that you're chomping at the bit to sell, let's go through the principles of pitching to the media and closing that deal, which is how we refer to getting your story into print.

Warming Up

FIRST, BE PREPARED. The fastest way for any PR professional to get off the ground is to prep for the pitch. Therefore, before you even consider picking up the phone, make sure you know your story inside and out. Have all the facts and figures at hand. Without the numbers, such as how much of your product has sold in the last month, quarter, or year; the percentage of increase you've experienced; or how many doughnuts your machine spurts out an hour; you've got zip. More than anything else, reporters hate being wrong about those factoids, and

E-Mail: The Subject of It All

En masse, the media have come to accept e-mail as their preferred communications tool. Pitching, planning, even video footage and B-roll (filmed background material)—all are shared over the digital wires. Unlike a phone call, e-mail lets you be direct and cut to the issue at hand. You don't have to ask how the kids are and what the weather's like; you just have to ask your question or get right to your pitch and press Send. There's no room for small talk in our lives, and there's even less room for it in your Outlook Inbox.

Now that we understand that the entire industry is sending, receiving, pinging, and ponging, how do you actually get journalists to read and consider your pitch via e-mail? Journalists penning well-read columns get an influx of a few hundred e-mail pitches a day, and 90 percent of them are surely garbage. Some of our friends who work in the media get so many junky e-mails that they don't even see ours sometimes. Understandably, then, they take their sweet time wading through these while working on other stories. The secret to getting yours opened, read, and considered is in those first viewed words in the under-remembered subject line. Hmm.

Mastering the subject line is becoming an art form. Look at your own inbox. Tricky marketers send subject lines that ruse you into opening their latest mortgage payment scheme or porn site. They put your first name in it (Subject: Bob! I Found Your Keys!), put your friend's name in it (Subject: Mary Thought You Would Like This), and offer wads of cash (Subject: Collect Your $5,000 And Don't Hesitate Or Else). Therefore, to intrigue smart journalists, who are faster on the delete key than the rest of the populace, you have to be not-at-all deceptive and a heck of a lot more creative.

When Mary Jane Journalist is rummaging through her e-mail inbox, she's searching for something to catch her eye. The type of thing that catches any journalist's eye is a subject line showing that you know what she covers, the ins and outs of her column or beat, and her particular style of thought.

Now, what about a story you know is perfect for a journalist, but you aren't sure how to get it in front of him? If you've worked with him, and even one pretty great story has come from the experience, stick your name right in there, "Subject: Mikey from RLM here." If those stories went as well as you think, your idea will get some play. For those who are always complaining about being too busy or never having enough time, try, "Subject: 30-Second Pitch." Who doesn't have half a minute? (For anyone who responds "me," we will tell you without hesitation to grow up real fast.)

Comedy goes a long way in the in-box, too. Anything four-or-so-words long that can get a chuckle will convince a journalist to dive deeper. In 2000, RLM put together a media barbecue with Amazon.com's Jeff Bezos (for discussion, see Chapter 4). Hell-bent on getting some beefy press coverage, we sent out e-mails with funny subjects, because the event itself was a bit of a joke. Lines like "Subject: Beers, Burgers and Bezos!" and "Subject: Jeff Bezos Has Great Buns" definitely caught the eye of the media, which has come to expect very buttoned-up transmissions from Jeff and his cronies.

Another tactic for subject line mastery comes straight from the 101 sales manuals. Remember, you're always closing, and instead of debating if a journalist should even meet with you, why not debate over the time and place? Then you can worry about wowing them in person. When we hit a city for a brief media tour, instead of shooting off e-mails with subject lines like "Subject: Fungible Audio Service Launches In D.C."—jeesh! How boring!—we send out e-mails with subject lines such as "Subject: Coffee Thursday." It's personal, it certainly makes them curious (did I forget to update my Outlook calendar?), and it propels the conversation straight to availability; we aren't even considering the announcement itself. This works, and it isn't manipulative. After all, I am e-mailing this book copy to my editor. She's paying attention. "Subject: Sorry I Am Late!"

you're the one supplying them. So get the facts straight.

Let's go backwards for a moment. When you make mistakes at work, the guy in the next cube probably knows, your smoke-break buddy definitely knows, and maybe, if the planets align against you, your boss finds out. That's bad enough, but if a journalist at the *New York Times* flounders, millions of people see the blunder, and that's tough to cover up! And *you* will surely get in trouble with that journalist. But even when your facts are totally correct, backing up your info with numbers from a source other than yourself will make an interested journalist at ease with the story and more willing to write it up.

The next thing you want to do after you're sure you can prove your theory or story with quantifiable data is to punch all the holes in it before someone else can. From the start, every ship is a leaky vessel. Before they roll a steamer into the harbor, they employ a team of pluggers in the hold to root out any bolts springing a leak and in need of tightening. Nothing's worse than having a journalist buy into your story and start reporting on it, only to leave it foundering out in open ocean. If they find too many variables in parts of the tale you're telling, the reporters will consider the concept you're pitching dead and consider you unreliable (or dead).

And when you leave the story for the media wolves, or when you get too caught up in your own story to see the holes in it, you have a pure PR nightmare. In 2001, rumors of a new vehicle, known as "IT" and "Ginger," buzzed through the media and into the pages of most of the country's daily papers and weekly magazines. Its inventor, Dean Kamen, is a modern-day mad scientist with a reputation for flying helicopters and taking jetpacks to his office. His inventions in the past were in the realm of medical science, among them a series of motorized wheelchairs that can balance on two wheels. He garnered a great deal of early acclaim, but when it came to IT/Ginger, Kamen stumbled on his own hype.

When Kamen began filing patents by the fistful for a transportation device, claiming that it would completely uproot the way major cities are mapped out, that it would be the most important development in personal mobility since the sandal (as his PR told it), and other colorful assertions, obviously the press took note. Harvard Business School Press reportedly paid a relatively unknown journalist a quarter of a million dollars to report on Ginger, on the strength of the hype.

Inquisitive journalists asked repeatedly if they could have a look, a test drive, or even a small quote, and Kamen refused every time. He did let buzz-laden pals like Jeff Bezos and uber-capitalist John Doerr of Kleiner Perkins Caufield & Byers go for a spin behind closed doors, and they whipped up plenty of hype about the upcoming Kamen adventure. "Amazing!" "A thrill-a-minute ride into the future!" "Nothing like it, ever." "I laughed, cried, and cheered."

The speculation got more and more intense. The media was sure Kamen was going to introduce the first hydrogen-powered contraption for everyday use, thereby saving the planet and all of civilization in a technological display of genius. When the big day came, the inventor shared his ambition on *Good Morning America,* where Charles Gibson himself took the first public ride on what was called the Segway Personal Transportation Device. What was this but merely a self-balancing, battery-powered dork-mobile for pocket-protector geeks too lazy to amble? In seconds, the media community pounced on Deano for his gumption!

During the months that followed, papers, magazines, and TV programs scoffed at the scooter, making fun of it every chance they got. New York lawmakers even passed a law forbidding the Segway on sidewalks, or in the city for that matter, before it even rolled off the assembly line.

The problem was that Kamen believed his own hype way too much. He was so confident that the scooter, which he spent days and nights and OPM (other people's money) creating, was so fabulistic that no one would ever question its usefulness. When they did, he didn't have a compelling-enough answer.

Sealing Up the Holes in Your Hull

THINK OF KAMEN'S BLUNDER as a cautionary tale. In other words, try to think like a reporter before you pitch. Reporters are notoriously cynical, and to be honest, if you had their job, you would be, too. So you need to be one step (or ten) ahead of them. Play "devil's advocate." What are the first questions you're going to get? What are the questions that will make you uncomfortable, or that you don't have an answer for yet? As Kamen found out, you need to find the holes before the reporters find them for you.

More often than not, there are great answers to the questions, but only you will know them. And hemming and hawing is not going to help your case. A journalist working off nothing more than a quick pitch doesn't have real knowledge, any time, or enough interest to figure out the answers for you. What you think is the greatest happening since sliced toast is going to come down to no one ever finding out about it if you play your cards wrong.

Work through every angle and write the answers down so you have them close at hand. Next, get together the background information on you, your company, or your big idea. Like sealing up the holes in the hull of your story, you need to have the basics together so there's a foundation to whatever a journalist jots down. And whatever you do, don't pitch a story without any substance (see sidebar, "The Pitch That Cried Wolf").

This doesn't mean that you have to invest thousands in an overdesigned press kit. Journalists aren't wowed by four-color graphics, CD-ROMs, or even, in most cases, glossy photos. Reporters want two things: simplicity and accuracy. Stick with the basics. These include a neat folder with several of your best press releases; a backgrounder that describes the history and mission of your business on one page; a fact sheet that describes when the business was founded, how many people are involved, and who your partners are; and your contact information clearly spelled out in a nice, neat Times New Roman font.

If you already have a clip or two that aren't from a competing newspaper or magazine and that explain your story and message well, include them with the material. Put in a dash of biographical material about individuals on your management team who are crucial to the telling of the story. And voilà! You've baked a fairly decent press kit.

No matter how new and futuristic your gadget or business is, someone else is doing something pretty similar. Make sure you know who all of your competitors are before you pitch. For your own good (not merely for reporters), a competitive matrix demonstrates where you stand in the hazy crowd. That matrix is easy to build. All you need is a Web browser and a few hours of hard research, and soon you'll be able to discern what makes you different from the rest. Among other things, it prepares you for some of those zinger questions. For instance, you might find that three other businesses perform exactly the same service you do, eliminating your up-to-now biggest selling point! Or you could find strengths you didn't know you had. You could discover (wow!) that what you thought of as an unimportant add-on service is what makes you really special.

Now you know your story—where it falls flat and where it shines, what those competitors are doing, and what the answers are to the questions coming up on the horizon. You're ready to pick up the phone and get some ink!

Dialing for Coverage

THIS IS THE PART we like to think of as "dialing for coverage." Since you know how to spot the right journalists for the story, there's nothing but a phone call standing between you and those glossy press clips. This is where we close the deal. But— there's always a "but"—there are a few critical steps to doing it brilliantly.

First of all, understand that you've got about twenty seconds on the phone to get the go-ahead, or you go directly to dial tone.

The Pitch That Cried Wolf

There are only so many reporters covering the field or industry you play in, whether it's automotive technology, software, clothing, or architectural design. With time and experience, you will wind up speaking to them all one day—or their brethren. In a world of instant communication and shrinking inner circles, a PR person who cries wolf with a few off-the-mark pitches is blackballed in a hurry.

There's nothing the media dislikes more than vapor (a non-story), so don't pitch it. Click over to Business Wire (www.businesswire.com) or any of its ilk on a given day and you can count up hundreds of thousands of dollars spent propagating vapor news. "Small Company A Signs Agreement with About-to-Fold Company B" or "InterSlice Tech.com Launches Bleeding-Edge Customer Tracking Functionality." Find us a journalist who actually wants to write about topics like that (how do they affect anyone else besides the people who wrote the releases?) and we will tip our hats to that PR person (who has a reporter cousin, of course).

The danger in vapor is that it builds a name for you quickly. The wrong name. If you're dabbling in handheld technology, say, and you pitch Ken Li, well-known gadgetry journalist, on every software upgrade, he's going to learn very rapidly not to take seriously any pitch you send his way. Who cares? The danger is that when you have real news, the kind that matters, such as the launch of your new device that makes the iPac shake in its boots, Ken will not pay attention because you've proven yourself to be a vapor merchant.

Start by showing the same respect you expect to receive. Selling doesn't mean snowballing. We're not here to sucker a poor press guy into covering us just for our benefit alone. We want to give reporters thoughtful stories and great ideas so they call us back further down the road. Start by asking if they're busy or on deadline, and that you'll only take a few seconds. Those "few seconds"

Before you blast out a cluster bomb of e-mails or send that release over the wire, consider long and hard what's interesting about it. Is it fascinating just because you've spent three tireless months working on the content? Is it amazing because your latest noodling brings you one step closer to a competitor that no one's ever heard of? If that's the case, hold off and wait 'til you have something worthier of the presses; in other words, don't believe your own story too much.

Larger public companies are especially guilty of pushing vapor into the press. There's a theory out there, one we don't subscribe to, that if you don't have a steady, weekly stream of information crossing the wires—also known as "the machine"—your business's progress has sunk to an uncompetitive pace. Remember that with public companies, their news unfortunately engenders an article or two (unfortunately, because it makes the firm think that what they put out is urgent, and so it compels them to keep the vapor machine oiled).

Yet when this non-urgent-news-pushing firm truly has something worth chatting about, the press may not bite. Everyone at the firm scratches their heads and wonders why. But reporter types and analysts are glazed over from the hundreds of newsless missives shot through that PR cannon. And they are all too familiar with firms that cry wolf.

The take-away from all of this is that vapor works only rarely. For example, it did for Seinfeld. If what you desire is real, respected coverage continually, sit on the vapor ("CEO sneezed today!"), and don't put it out there. You'll only numb the reporters who should care and who should notice that what you do is important.

are the first test of timing. As the failed comedian said: "It's … all … about … timing …."

Technique is indeed crucial. Throughout the conversation you will want the journalist to keep saying yes and giving you indicators to continue. If you simply ask if he's busy and don't say anything further, he'll always say yes, and you're done. If you say it will only take a few seconds, you'll get the okay to proceed, and you'd better make it fast because the reporter is as busy as you think. What you're doing is getting the reporter to say yes. "Yes" lets you proceed. "Yes" closes stories. Look for the "yes" label. (By all means, don't ask him to point you in the right direction in terms of pitching the story. We'd hang up on you, too.)

Now we're into the thick of the pitch—we're selling, baby. To sell anything takes a real sense of enthusiasm. You've picked up the phone late at night to the sound of an unenthusiastic credit card or newspaper pitch. Every time you hear it, you cut the telemarketer off. A friend of mine pretends he's died. Whatever. Anyway, the point of all this is that even if the telemarketer might be saving you huge interest payments or offering a free car wash for listening, you don't want to hear it. They aren't into it, so you aren't, either.

The same is true for media relations. You can offer a journalist an exclusive interview with God, but if you aren't excited about the idea, God may lose a believer. You have to be energized that you're on the phone with the journalist and excited about whatever it is you're pitching. Now, there's a difference between liveliness and artificiality. Don't be a phony. Just be charming.

Easy Does It

CONTROLLING THE PACE is the next step to advancing the conversation in the direction you want it to go. If you carry on in a hurried proclamation, you're going to make the journalist (or anyone else, for that matter) uneasy and hurried, too. Take your time. Be relaxed, cool. If you take the urgency out of the call, the person at the other end feels a bit more "breezy," too.

Next, relate the story to the journalist in plain English, minus the trade or industry jargon. And remember to whom you're talking. In other words, there's a reason you have *that journalist* there with you, and not a reporter in a different department or on the opposite side of the country. At the other end of the phone is the match for your story! Let her know that, and why she's the perfect fit for your story.

You might have heard of a junior New York business magazine called *Empire NY*. We reached out to muster some great coverage for its 2002 launch; our goal was to let sassy business types know this stylish pub was there, waiting to be devoured. The first people we called were reporters and local broadcast media with a metro beat. The opening line of the pitch wasn't, "We're launching a new magazine, Mr. Producer at NY1 News. We think you'll dig it."

It went more like this: "Hey, Mr. Producer, we've got the New York story of the week for you! Do you have a few seconds? It's absolutely worth it. Yes? Great! *Empire NY,* a new magazine just for New York, is about to canvass the city on Thursday, and it's got everyone talking already. It's about money, power, and celebrities, and the publisher can tell you and the viewers about it Wednesday morning—before it hits the shelves and all the media writers pick up on it."

Let's highlight a couple of things here. First, it's all e-n-e-r-g-y and a ton of hype. But there's nothing wrong with hype, as long as you're smart about using it (see the Dean Kamen parable above). Money, power, and celebrities are New York's (or anybody's) three favorite things, and no one can turn them down. Also, the pitch conveys a sense of urgency, as in, "Move it, Mr. Producer." Mr. P. was told he could speak to the publisher before the media writers get their hands on a brand-new magazine. That gives him something special to latch on to, particularly since magazine launches are pretty rare in these digital days. We made him feel as if he's getting something extra; let's call it a scoop!

Last, notice that we gave the producer a specific time and date. This is critical, because it is primarily a call to action. If you don't set dates and times, nothing happens. You need to close, not let things hover in the air. "We will see you Wednesday at 9:00 A.M. at Coffee Bar Dolce." That's it.

Nothing's worse than leaving a good pitch unresolved with the media because they move on to the Next Big Thing. Then you spend the next month trying to reignite their interest. The second reason you have to make a date is that you're more likely to get a yes, assuming this time works for Mr. P. The discussion becomes about scheduling only, not the magazine.

And once you're scheduled, you are good like gold money. You want the opportunity to get the product in front of him to answer questions, rather than haphazardly meander around the details over a brief pitch call. If the time you offer is out of the question, try another one. What about asking Mr. P. what time is better— mornings, afternoons, the end of the week? You're rounding third base, getting them to wave you home. Pitch ... Bunt ... Steal ....

You're outta here! Okay, it didn't work. What happened was that Mr. Producer wasn't so easy, and he wanted to hear what's really so great about this magazine with the funny title. Mr. P. explained calmly that he already gets *Crain's New York Business* every week, and that suited his business tastes just fine. This is where the prep work pays off. Even though we like *Crain's*, we needed to *kinda* pan it to close the deal.

You're on Third; the Bases Are Loaded...

"*CRAIN'S* IS GREAT; my grandfather's been reading it for thirty years because he fears change." Now you could sense a flicker of interest from Mr. P. "*Crain's* is fantastic for a stodgy real estate tycoon," we continued, "but people like you or me, who want to find out who's making big money and how—*and* where the best martinis in town are—will go for the stylish and hands-on *Empire NY*. I can have a B-roll of the first issue coming off the presses for you by Tuesday night for a Wednesday morning shoot."

He's still wavering (sigh) ... so we go for broke: "Look, Mr. P., People watch NY1 because they want to know about New York, not D.C. That's the same reason they'll read

Empire, too. It's a logical match. It's not right for Fox, so don't make me send it there."

Now he's been handed an ultimatum—a subtle one, but it's definitely been put out there. It's a damned good story for him, and he knows it. We also gave it to him very early, with some B-roll footage to make his production a little snappier (allowing him to keep his self-filming cameras in the office). Suddenly this is a cheap, easy-to-accomplish, and good-looking segment for Mr. P.

Sometimes, rather than stride into home plate, you have to take *off* the kid gloves and push the Mr. P.'s of the world up against the dugout wall! As we've said throughout the whole book, if you *desire the coverage you deserve,* please remember: It's always easier for Mr. Producer or any reporter *not* to do the story, so you've got to let him know he's missing out and that someone else will pick it up on the next PR call. Smart journalists appreciate your candor.

You've scored: Mr. P. wants the story, so now you really have to get to work. Just because he says yes doesn't mean you're done. The job isn't over until the piece airs. You have to FedEx *all* the information you have on *Empire NY* right away. Make sure that the video footage you promised is there when you said it would be, too. You can also help by typing up some quick, bulleted conversation points for him, so that during the segment, he asks relevant questions. Anything Mr. P. asks for, he gets, because if it becomes too much work for him, you're not making it to the small screen.

If the production process or article goes well, always send a handwritten thank-you note (see commandment number two below) to the journalist or producer, not to thank him for the coverage—you gave him a great story and it's his job to cover it—but because you enjoyed working with him. If you did a good job, you can be sure that your card also made it into his Rolodex or Palm Pilot.

When you pitch stories to the press, the important thing to

know is that to be a good PR person and a great pitcher, you don't have to be a corporate spokesperson and spinmeister, which is what everyone assumes. You simply need to be the one person who levels with the media and tells journalists the way it is, honestly and clearly. Some people who can't do PR are stubborn folks, those who think they know it all and can do no wrong. These people don't succeed because they put themselves in harm's way. As with any insider game, there's an understood etiquette with the media, an unspoken set of rules, by which you need to abide when you're pitching stories and working with the media in general. Here are the most important ones for you to take to heart. Ignore them at your peril.

Thou Shalt Not Lie—
and 27 Other Media Relations Do or Die Commandments

1 **Don't bribe journalists.** If your story isn't good enough for the media, or if your pitch isn't hitting home, regroup, fix the problem, and patch all the holes. Bribing a journalist is buying your way into the publication, and if that's what you want, make life easier for both of you and buy an advertisement. The best way to get a journalist to take your story is to prepare and hone the pitch so it delivers your message and addresses the media's real needs.

2 **If you're happy with the way a story turns out, don't send a gift thanking the reporter.** Your intentions may be perfectly honorable, but once again, a gift is problematic for a journalist. All you're doing is putting her ethics up for debate, because if she ever chooses to cover you in the future, a case can be made that you *endeared* your way in. Send a handwritten note expressing what a pleasure it was to work with her. That's best. It'll take longer to get there than a call or an e-mail, but it's the way to go. Also, if you decide to take a reporter out for dinner, discuss who pays for the meal beforehand. It's much simpler and more clear-cut for everyone.

3   **Strike the word *favor* from your media relations vocabulary.**
You hear it day in and day out—PR and business people saying that they'll make a call because so-and-so at this paper
owes them a favor. Eliminate the notion that the media owes
you anything, and your expectations will be manageable. Just
because you gave a reporter a story once, and he covered it
once, doesn't mean he owes you. (And the silly notion that
someone did something "bad" to you in print or neglected to
include you, and that you therefore merit something wonderful in the future—pshaw ... drop it.)

In most lines of work, you can offer favors, at least tiny
ones, such as free parking in the office lot, gratis use of a
spiffy electronic device, and so on. But asking journalists to
cover something just because you gave it to them is asking
them to compromise the very product they make and distribute to thousands of their own consumers. Any journalist
or producer is way too far out in the spotlight and, theoreti-
cally, too ethical, to compromise his product to pay you back
for a supposed favor.

4   **Don't let your boss or colleagues tell you that they'll handle getting the media coverage if you're the one with the
connections.** You've gone to great pains to build the media
relationship, so you should decide the best way to deal with
someone. Friends in the media? Sure, that's a reality. But a
friend, secondhand? Rarely, if ever. What your higher-
up thinks is a friend usually is someone he talked to at a
cocktail party.

Time and time again, a client has beseeched us not to
talk to a reporter because she, thinking she had an "in" with
the reporter, was going to handle it herself. And every single
time, either we've had to step in to clean up the mess, or the
reporter, with whom we've had a longstanding relationship,
has called us to say, "Why is this person bugging me?" It's
nothing personal. A friend, it's said, "is someone you don't

owe anything to." Tell the CEO you'll handle it because you want to do your job well.

5 **Don't believe that whatever you're doing is too important to disclose.** Entrepreneurs, inventors, and generic know-it-alls always seem to be in a very unhealthy form of "stealth mode," tediously toiling away on their next big idea in a locked lab guarded by nondisclosure agreements. But, of course, they want to be famous, too. The first thing to remember is that no matter what you're doing, provided it isn't curing cancer or AIDS, someone else is doing something more important than you are.

As a nation we were duly reminded of this when, in mid-2002, Secretary of State Colin Powell left each meeting at the supposed "pre-peace talks" anticipating, for the benefit of the press, what the next meeting would be like, without granting one detail of the prior meeting. Dull, misinforming, and self-important. If the media wants to know about it (because *you* called *them,* remember?), then give them the full story. Never solicit coverage and then give only half the news. It's pretentious and off-putting.

Anyway, if the idea *is* that great, it will take years before anyone's able to replicate it. Plus, the mere fact that you're first makes you the best. If it is that easy to copy, then maybe it's not such a good idea, after all.

6 **Don't miss a deadline.** Don't miss a deadline. Oh, and one more thing: Don't miss a deadline. The media live and die by the clock. If you're working with a reporter on your story, always make her schedule yours. If you're late with information, she's late with the story to her editor. This makes her look bad, and then the space in the paper or broadcast that was reserved for her story will have to be filled quickly, and then the whole production goes up in smoke. That means your next chance (or three) with the reporter goes up in smoke, too. *It is always easier to kill a story than to write one.*

All right, let's say you did miss the deadline. Here's when we say to 'fess up quick. Despite all your attempts to put your best foot forward, you've screwed up, but whatever you do, don't let that story die. Try a little tenderness and apologize to the frustrated reporter (and mean it).

What can you do to make it better, you ask? E-mail or fax a note that she can show her editor, one that explains the problem and acknowledges your responsibility in causing it. If you can still come through with the information by the publication's deadline, move mountains to do it. And, of course, promise never to miss a deadline again. Can you keep that one?

7 **Don't pitch one of your stories that just appeared in a competing newspaper or magazine and pretend you didn't see it or have anything to do with it.** When that little fib comes back to haunt you—and it will—ouch, does that smart! It's true that not everyone at the *New York Times* reads the *Wall Street Journal,* and vice versa. On the other hand, the *Wall Street Journal* swears *BusinessWeek* is its prime competitor, and each member of its reporter team studies it like the dickens. Therefore, it's a big mistake to think that the reporter won't notice that the same story you're pitching just showed up on the competition's front page.

Even if he doesn't notice, do yourself a favor and avoid getting into this situation to begin with. If a journalist who doesn't know better buys into your story and presents it to his editor, he's in for some serious trouble, and so are you. Honesty is the name of the game; you'll never win a reporter's trust with deceptive tactics.

That doesn't mean that you can't pitch to two competing papers if you have a timely story. Journalists won't always get back to you when they promise to or run your story when they were planning to—or ever, for that matter. The important thing to remember is that if one writer from the *Times* bites, you should let his alter ego at the *Journal* know that up front. If you're honest about it with the *Journal* scribe, you ensure that his editor won't beat him up for running a day-late, dollar-short scoop.

If you're really good at this PR stuff, you could give him an opportunity to cover your story from a different angle. You could also tell him not to cover it at all if the whole issue becomes too sticky. In any case, the next time you call your pal at the *Journal,* he'll know you're a pro. And that's what counts with reporters.

Sometimes two competing journalists will run the same story, and they *both* get heat for it. In this instance, the best thing to do is offer a very humble apology and take their wrath on the chin. What's done is done. Walking the ethical side of the line in PR will get you far, even when you make mistakes. In an industry filled with wonderful one-hits and people trying to make a name for themselves doing all sorts of weird things, rules of conduct are always broken. He who treads safely will stand out and gain influence over the long haul.

8 **Don't break a deal.** If you offer a reporter an exclusive, make sure it stays an exclusive. If you set up a press embargo for Friday, don't try to change the date to Monday or Tuesday later on. Success in PR is based on verbal agreements, so honor them, and there will be more deals for you to close in the future.

9 **Never lie.** Don't even exaggerate. This one doesn't need much explanation, other than to reiterate that lying about a product or service makes a journalist who reports it look like a dolt. Not to mention the obvious ethical problem on your end. Don't do it! But if it does happen, if you or someone in your company does lie, well then, call back, apologize, and make amends quickly. Say the devil made you do it, if you have to.

10 **Don't give journalists only one option for using your story.** If you are collaborating with a reporter on one angle, and it isn't working, don't just sigh and say, "Ah well, maybe next time." Find angles anew—there are always more. If you don't, you may as well just sit around and wait for the reporter to kill the piece, and with it, your opportunity for press coverage.

11 **Don't ever believe that you can say anything off the record.** If you don't want to read it the next morning in the paper, don't say it. Many people like to exchange off-the-record quips with journalists to buddy up to them. But you are only creating problems for the writer when you spill dirty little secrets. Here's why: Journalists don't have to honor off-the-record statements. Their job is to report the news, and if your off-the-record scoop is news, they need to tell it.

But it's not quite that simple for a journalist. He has to decide whether to break your trust and run with the information or spend his day trying to find three or four other sources to validate your rumor. Either way, it's a lot of work for him, and he doesn't really want to be in that position, anyway. So do yourself and the journalist a favor: Don't go there.

12 **Never say that you don't know, or that you can't answer a question.** Just don't. *No comment* is a product of Hollywood. It's an incriminating answer: By not commenting, you're saying a whole lot. If you aren't comfortable disclosing something, segue to safer territory (see Chapter 6, "It's YOUR Interview!") and tell the inquisitive reporter that when you have the answer to the question, she's the first one you'll call with the information.

If she asks you a question on a subject you can't talk about it, such as a legal or Securities and Exchange Commission issue, tell her so. If your hands are tied—you'd get sued or thrown in jail for talking too soon—then you have to explain it just like that. Acting coy is not a good idea here.

13 **Don't leave voice messages and e-mail unanswered.** If you want serious press, you must be accessible and helpful. Never leave the media hanging, waiting for you to get back to them. If you do, they'll just move on to the next story they're working on. You'll only get calls if you return them!

If you're truly swamped and cannot answer, ask someone from your office to call and say, "She's truly swamped and cannot get back to you today, but she does want to speak with you. So how's midnight tonight for you?" You'll get a chuckle on the other end of the line, but you'll have scored points for making an honest effort to be accessible.

14 **Never be egotistical.** Even if you're the person being interviewed, it's not all about you. If your ego gets in the way of your story, journalists won't want to deal with you, and if the story actually *does* make it to press, rest assured that they would use sarcasm to describe you and your big idea. Definitely not what you're after.

15 **Don't play hard-to-get with your answers.** Journalists are looking for straight facts, and great PR people are only too happy to supply the answers. The idea isn't to be a spin-meister, weaving a web of confusion, but to be there to answer questions and get a story in print. All of the facts discussed may not be beneficial to you, but they're probably quite necessary for the whole of the story.

16 **Don't make a sport out of getting the upper hand on the media.** Some people feel strongly that "us versus them" is the way to play the game. Don't be that way. Everyone has a job to do. If you feel you need to have the upper hand with someone, you're doing it wrong. You're there to help the reporter fill the giant, gaping hole in his story by supplying all that great information about your company. The idea is *not* to be a giant thorn in his side, so don't play games at all. And if you feel a game coming on, go home and take an aspirin.

17 **Expunge buzzwords and jargon from your vocabulary.** Don't even *think* about using them. Using industry-speak or buzzwords is surely the quickest way to make the media (and everyone else) glaze over with boredom. The venerable *New York Times* is written for the comprehension level of an eleven-year-old. Make sure that what you say is easy to understand and doesn't require a five-minute explanation. Your sole job is to make things simple, so don't let language be your downfall. Take to heart the sweet words of Oscar Wilde: "Simply edit, my dear."

Sometimes it helps to try out words on friends. We say ask your local teenagers whether they have a clue about what you mean—they're a little older than the *New York Times* reading level, but they'll do. And, of course, you can always ask yourself in the mirror, like we do: What am I *really* trying to say? How can I say it more quickly and clearly?

18 **Simply do not let the media walk all over you.** You are not a doormat. Journalists are like anyone else, and if you let them walk all over you, they will. Set some guidelines and let them know you aren't a pushover. You're there to contribute your share of a mutually beneficial relationship. If it doesn't seem to be a two-way street, get off at the next exit. As Cindy Crawford once muttered about men, journalists are like trains; you can always find another one coming 'round the bend.

19 **Don't let the media put words in your mouth.** Ensure that journalists and producers infer what you imply. Sometimes our words can be understood differently from how we intend them, so be certain you're explaining yourself clearly and be positive that the media understands your meaning.

If, in fact, you did explain yourself clearly, and the interview that's published or broadcast is inaccurate or misleading, call the producer or reporter and try to make the point again. The media can correct or retract statements that hurt you and your company. If you are dead set on a correction or retraction, make your case boldly, and show them that you mean business.

20 **Don't think like everyone else, because you'll always be viewed as "regular."** The way to get real coverage is to be grand, bigger than the rest and willing to say the unexpected. Take the same collection of facts that everyone else sees and assemble them with pizzazz! Looking at the world through PR-colored glasses takes practice, but seeing the other side of the world, and disclosing what you've found, builds the big buzz. In general, it pays to be cultured, knowledgeable, somewhat well rounded, and—not normal. You want to be memorable when you're making calls and sending e-mails to those who receive thousands of them daily.

21 **Don't shoot down your media opportunities by thinking your big idea isn't doable.** Just about anything in the world is doable. To cite one small example, Barbra Streisand played a thirteen-year-old when she was forty-one! Just as long as the authorities aren't involved and you aren't slogging around in the depths of moral turpitude, you're set. A smart PR guy once told us that the best way to approach PR was to try to figure out how to get your logo on the next orbit-bound space shuttle and work it from there. If you set your sights high, your fortunes will follow, and so will the camera crews!

22 **Don't miss an opportunity to participate in the larger story.** Always read and watch the news if you're trying to be a part of it. There's always a bigger trend to keep an eye on, and maybe your small business or big idea is relevant to the conversation. That's your "in"! Jump on it, make the calls, and become part of the news. Just remember: Staying informed is the key to being a part of the big picture.

23 **Don't let ornery journalists discourage you.** We have a saying in our business: "The smaller they are ... the smaller they are." (You probably can figure that one out on your own.)

Look, you're going to get plenty of no's. That doesn't mean a thing. Patrick Dennis, writer of the megahit novel *Auntie Mame,* sent it to about a hundred publishers—when there were that many (sigh)—before someone decided to pay him a pittance to make that book appear. The rest is history.

No matter how good your pitch or story is, you'll get more no's than yeses. That's just the way it goes. Know that for each no you get, though, there's a yes right around the corner. It only takes one story to get the ball rolling. Most PR professionals hate pitching, because most people are just plum worn down by rejection. Rejection will always be a part of the sales routine. You can't take it personally. It was the story they said no to, not you, but if you go in there intent on closing and you really want it, you'll get a lot fewer no's than everybody else.

The point of this comment—not to be New Agey here—is that you are going to be the one to make "the story" a reality. Waiting for your mobile to ring is a clear indication that you will be a victim. Every one of us has had bad days in the PR world. So what? My grandmother used to tell me: "Float five things up in the air and some will fall and others will stay aloft." It's a bizarre, somewhat old-world philosophy, but ... it works!

24 **Don't think a news outlet is too small for your great idea.** Remember what Gloria Swanson said in *Sunset Boulevard:* "It's the pictures that got small!" Day in and day out, our clients say they don't want to waste their time speaking with *Wireless Review, Call Center* magazine, or atNewYork.com because they're too small or no one reads them. Press begets press, darn it, and if you turn coverage down, you've set yourself up to fail. The big secret is that most journalists read the small news outlets like atNewYork.com to find great stories before they hit the mainstream. Do you think they dream up all those stories on their very own?

25 **Never go to an interview without an agenda.** And don't try to fake it, because when you mess up you'll smack yourself squarely in the forehead. Before you talk to the media, you should know what you want to say and what the story is. Going in without an agenda will lead to a conversation with no direction and no story because there isn't one thought for the journalist to zero in on. Be focused and get that message out at any given (or earned!) opportunity.

26 **If you are on national TV, and you feel like making an off-color joke, don't.** Even if you think that somehow it will ingratiate you with the host or hostess, don't. Particularly if it's about another guest, no matter how light-hearted it is, just don't. You'll never get asked back. Other producers who are watching will scratch you off their lists, too.

27 You've been so perfectly behaved throughout this chapter that we decided to add one more commandment, the one that truly counts: **Don't say no to all these *ixnays*.** They are time-tested and worth paying attention to. Use and obey!

CHAPTER 6

It's YOUR Interview!

WHATEVER THE SITUATION, a media interview serves one purpose for you: It's a forum for delivering your key messages about yourself, your product, your company, or your big idea. From a reporter's point of view, of course, it is also an information-gathering exercise. Think of an interview as a chess game, and always play to win.

Every principle in this chapter is designed to help you accomplish one paramount objective: Control that interview. We say "your" interview because you own it, not the reporter. Approach the interview with the idea in mind that you are leading the cause. The media will "dig" what you have to say as long as you give the journalist a story—a real, honest-to-goodness piece of information that indeed tells the listener something he didn't know before. That's what we call earning press coverage ... you know, earnestly.

The Confidence Game

LET'S START BY SETTING the stage for a fab interview. In the two decades we've been in the media game, we've identified the one important quality that all of the most notable newsmakers have and that struggling spokespersons lack: real confidence. Most of the people we've worked with to date have been brilliant minds— innovators, entrepreneurs, and successful businesspeople with a keen sense of themselves.

They're huge personalities at the top of their games. They've convinced the staunchest bankers to fork over millions of dollars to fund their venture, persuaded the best executives to give up secure jobs to take a spin on their roller-coaster ride, and swayed millions of consumers to buy their wares. They're chiefly sales-men among salesmen, capable of selling binoculars to the blind.

But when it came to selling the story to the media, most of them couldn't do it—at first. In the throes of an interview, most people in the hot seat lose whatever charisma they've got. They choke, get defensive, squirm in their chairs, and foul up valuable opportunities that will not come their way again. Broadcast inter-views are the most intensely challenging. No matter how weath-ered an executive is, when the cameras start rolling, so do beads of sweat from the brow.

Confidence in front of the camera is a precious resource, but unlike platinum and rhino horns, it can definitely be culti-vated and eventually honed into a fine skill that you can write home about. Bright lights and live TV will no longer turn your stomach and force you into giving a performance that you regret later. Just learn how to use the tools. Educate yourself so that you can take any situation and turn it into an opportunity to deliver your message—clearly, accurately, with pizzazz. See, with the press you have only one chance to get it right. There's no time for freezing up in front of the camera. The average television interview lasts only a few minutes (often seconds), and it takes lots of practice to explain the benefits of what you're offering in that short amount of time.

What you need to do first is to keep the power balance in perspective. Journalists are required to report news and information on one or two topics. But that doesn't mean that they are experts. The science behind manufacturing, logistics, wireless communications, or whatever your field is changes daily. If a journalist completely understood your industry, he wouldn't dedicate his day to listening to and learning from you, would he? Suffice it to say that you are the expert, and members of the media are not.

Therefore, be confident in what you do, and let that translate into what you say to the press. You are there to enlighten others. That's what a pro thinks as he starts off any interview—no matter with whom, where, or why. Pure salesmanship has no limits.

Practice Makes Perfect

NOW THAT YOU'RE in the right frame of mind, the next step before you go on that debut interview is to prep yourself. Know exactly what message you want to deliver, and focus on getting it out there as much, as quickly, and as solidly as anyone could. And your laundry list of messages should be a short one. Don't dither, ramble, or use long, convoluted sentences. Use basic words in the English language, and spit it right out.

We also tell our clients to stay focused. One-on-one time with journalists is scarce, and time on TV is even shorter. Getting caught up in small talk will bring whatever momentum you might have achieved to a grinding halt. You could equate an interview to a service at a gospel church. The line of questioning is like call and response, and you need to be the caller, not the responder.

Here's what we mean. Just like a first date, a journalist sitting across from you at a local Starbucks is going to break the ice

Tips for Radio and TV Interviews

*Any good PR person can tell you that TV is easy. But for many peo-
ple, this is something they have to learn for themselves. You are the
star, and even if you're nervous, remember that this is something
you can do well, because you're talking about your all-time favorite
subject: your product or company.*

*The host or producer will usually conduct a "pre-interview" for
a few minutes before you go on the air. The pre-interview is important because it establishes what is expected of you on the air and
the direction the interview will take. It is also your chance to tell the
interviewer what you would like to discuss.*

*For radio and television, you should know beforehand when the
interview will take place and how long it will last. Since there are
often last-minute changes, ask the interviewer to tell you when the
interview will begin. Shows have begun without the guest being
aware of it, and off-the-cuff remarks, never intended for public consumption, have reached the ears of listeners, with embarrassing and
damaging results.*

Everything on radio and television is timed. Keep your answers

with some offhand remark about the weather, or critique of the
public transportation or highway that got her there. It sounds
banal, but a simple opening question like "How's it going?" is the
gateway to success or failure in an interview, because it is the first
test of your ability to focus on creating buzz for your product.

So ... how *is* it going? In 2002, LookSmart, one of the
biggest marketers on the Web, purchased WiseNut, a super-hot
search engine primed to take down Google, another popular
search engine. If a journalist were to ask Evan Thornley,
LookSmart's jolly chairman, how things were going at that point
in time, he would immediately declare, "Great! We just purchased
the technology needed to make a Google search look like a ran-

short and concise, or the interviewer will interrupt you before you are able to make your point. Most answers should be no longer than three or four sentences. Here are some other tips:

❑ *Wear conservative clothing for television interviews. (Okay, sometimes it is about the color of your shirt.) A white shirt and navy-blue or gray suit are favorites for men in the news business. Women should wear solid colors and subtle makeup and jewelry.*

❑ *Remember that the camera may be on you during a television interview even if you're not talking. Make a special effort to control your gestures and expressions.*

❑ *Sit still and erect but relaxed, especially in a studio interview. A slight lean forward conveys energy and a positive attitude. Don't swivel, rock, lean, slump, or swing your legs. Don't clasp your hands or grip your chair, and don't grind your teeth or tighten and loosen your jaw. That's tough when you're angry or worried about something, so make up with your colleagues and loved ones before interviews, and try to put yourself in an upbeat state of mind, even if it's only for the duration of the interview.*

dom selector machine." If Thornley made a general reply, such as "Everything is going fine," or merely joined in on everyone's favorite mass transit gripe, he would forfeit an opportunity to "be calling," which in this case means turning the conversation in the direction he wanted to take it, to LookSmart's dynamic new deal. Instead, he would be responding.

Taking control requires the confidence needed to succeed, but it generates even more confidence, giving you even more poise for future interviews: It's a symbiotic relationship. Keeping the conversation revolving around your topic and your message gives you the edge, and the familiar ground should support your self-assurance.

It's Not What You Say ....

REPETITION BUILDS RETENTION, so the more you say it, the more it will stick. On the other hand, you don't want to blurt out a rehearsed one-liner, either. Politicians say the same thing over and over, word for word, and we don't trust them. The only other people who lock themselves into repetition are people who are uncomfortable talking outside a script—or, more likely, people who have something to hide.

Instead, what you want is to be able to say the same thing over and over, but in a different way each time. Always use a story, because stories paint pictures worth thousands of words. A good vignette makes your product relevant and brings your point home.

In February 2000, days before the e-conomy fell like a heavy stone, Seth Goldstein, late-twenty-something entrepreneur at the venture capital firm Flatiron Partners, sat across the table from Tony Guida on CNN. Seth was there to explain why he had $50 million in his pocket earmarked for "pervasive computing" and what, exactly, pervasive computing was. (In case you're wondering, we'll get to the definition in a moment.) Seth's task was to explain why pervasive was so hot, and why he was the guy to fund the next big idea. But he had a big hurdle to overcome: Pervasive computing is a simple concept, but few people can explain it in simple terms.

Yet there was Seth, on TV, doing just that. He made it simple to understand for the millions watching CNN that night, because he explained it countless times, and each explanation was different from the last. He began by defining pervasive computing as the shift away from Web content on the PC and onto specific devices. The journalist asked him to explain a bit more, so Seth rephrased the definition: He said that it was a continuous experience that, with the Internet, ensured that devices other than your computer would deliver the capabilities of the Web to you. From the bathroom to the boardroom, the Web would be in your pocket, giving you the info you need exactly when and where you need it.

Seth used his confidence—artificial and otherwise—to make the concepts real with some fun examples. Tiny, pervasive computing devices could be built into your fridge, for example, that knew when you were out of milk and ordered a new carton for you. Or perhaps the pervasive device knows that you like the Knicks, not the Nets, and it has an inkling of the type of stocks you trade and gives you the information you want on the subjects that matter the most to you.

Indeed, Seth made Guida all hot and bothered with an explanation of the new, digital picture frame that displayed photos found on Web pages and an Internet radio that played music like a regular radio, except that the tunes come from the Web, not from the airwaves. At the end of those four minutes (and four minutes is a luxury on television, by the way) everyone watching CNN that night "got" what pervasive computing was. Seth put it in terms that everyone could relate to, over and over again. The conversation was about his topic, so his confidence was soaring. He owned the show, and everyone who was watching that night.

The question you may be asking yourself right about now is: What if the topic turns toward something you aren't comfortable with? A few years back, my cohort Michael Prichinello spent some time as the communications director for New York's Lt. Governor Betsy McCaughey Ross. His experience as the mouthpiece for a firecracker politician taught him the delicate science of directing the conversation and making it your own.

Far from the civil number two she was expected to be, Betsy was a loose cannon, challenging the old boys' network whenever the opportunity presented itself. In the chaotic seas of New York politics, Betsy's outlaw actions made her an island on the fringe of the map. She crossed party lines, publicly attacked party members, and even challenged her own governor in the election—sure political suicide.

During her reign, Mike had the tough job of delivering Betsy's platform on issues such as the expansion of health care to cover procedures deemed "experimental" but necessary (like bone-marrow and stem-cell transplants) and the passage of gun control laws to reduce the number of New York toddlers involved in accidental household shootings. But all the media wanted to talk about was her public feud with Governor Pataki, the breakup of her two-year-old marriage to financier Wilbur Ross, and the $10 million missing from her campaign war chest.

So Mike quickly learned how to use two staples of public relations, bridging and flagging (discussed in more detail later in this chapter). When these two techniques are used properly, there isn't a conversation out there you can't master with ease. Bridging is merely using a phrase that gets you from Topic A, or one that you aren't confident in or don't want to discuss, to Topic B, the one you really want to discuss right now.

For example, Mike was on the phone with a venomous political journalist who asked if Betsy slept in the office to avoid seeing her husband at home. He was hot on the trail of a controversial tell-all, but all Mike wanted to talk about was health care reform! He needed to bridge to turn the conversation back to his own turf. His response was, "You should know that here in Albany, Betsy vowed not to sleep until everyone suffering from cancer got a check from their insurance company ..."

Thus the stage was set to talk about health care again, and the journalist got the point: Mike wasn't going to help with this sensationalist angle. At that moment, the pause he needed was installed, and Mike was able to continue talking about Betsy's health care platform again, spurting facts and figures to support her position.

During Mike's time with this colorful politico, he kept notes for phone interviews that mapped out the different paths he would take to get out of a mess—that is, back to familiar ground. As he got better at it and gained some confidence, the notes started to disappear. There is a special power in knowing how to handle yourself well in an interview, a power to which people naturally gravitate.

Speak Your Mind—Fiercely

CAPTURE THAT CONFIDENCE. It sells, it mesmerizes, and it makes people appear larger than life (well, in the press, anyway). Producers always tell us they need to "see" an air of confidence for on-air types. Confident guests make for great TV. And great TV means you get called back. Face it: You're available, you're good, and you know the way to the studio! And confident folks say the unexpected, they swagger, they aren't afraid to rock the boat, and they get their point across.

Oh, and do we have to say it? They're not boring.

During the summer of 2000, a site that started off as the hobby for Web programmer Philip Kaplan became a media darling. Philip registered the URL www.FuckedCompany.com as a lark to track the downfall of digital companies for entertainment. Word of the website spread like wildfire from cubicle to cubicle, and the media picked up on the hype.

Suffice it to say that any website bent on telling readers about those who were once rich and famous and who were now getting "theirs" was going to be popular in the wayward year 2000. But initially Philip's interviews bordered on disastrous. He was visibly shaken on camera; his nervous twitches, lack of focus, and overall awkwardness scarred his performance.

After a few practice runs, though, Pud, as he is nicknamed, began to realize that what journalists wanted most were those secret tips he was receiving from thousands of followers. They wanted information that he had; that was his power. Philip began to feel more secure in his skin, and his comments became wittier. Plainly, before everyone's eyes, he started to gain control of the conversations. The more his performance improved, the more producers called him to appear as that day's guest.

Fully aware of what the coverage was doing for his website traffic and personal profile, Philip took his on-air persona to the next level. After a few trips to Versace, he began dressing like a boardroom rock star. To put it mildly, the media couldn't get enough. He was everywhere, from CNN *Moneyline* to the cover of *Inc.* to MTV. His newfound confidence made him the star—the media all wanted a piece of him!

But you may be surprised to learn that Philip wasn't parting with particularly provocative data or even shedding light on something his readers didn't know. The truth is, dying dot-coms were stale before the message ever got to the media. The real point is that he got coverage because he was completely confident in himself, and nothing was going to stop him from showing off!

Confidence, although artificial at first, eventually breeds a real sense of self. Like most things in business, media relations are about sales. But you're not just selling products to viewers and readers: You're selling yourself to the media, too. Journalists and producers want and need strong personalities every day—people who have answers and drip with confidence. Self-assured people become confidants to journalists, who feel that those with confidence, whether learned or innate, are also secure enough to say what they're thinking, not what they think people expect them to say.

As we said earlier, you're the expert at what you do; that's what got you the interview in the first place. Speak your mind, fiercely. Have no fear. This is not speaking in front of a crowd. It's speaking to an audience of one. No matter how outlandish your statements might sound, if you believe it, that's all you need. Confident delivery automatically gives any statement a certain amount of credibility. And since that's what the press wants, give it to them. They'll come back for more. And more.

Being a big personality in the news makes even the most cynical people notice, especially producers and reporters who have seen you. You'll find that your swagger will pay off. Once you have more confidence in yourself, the press will, too.

Okay, you're raring to go, and you're ready to face the cameras, or at least a journalist or two. Now you're going to learn how to give a reporter a "dy-no-mite!" interview, à la Jimmy 'J. J.' Walker from the TV show *Good Times*.

How to Give a "Dy-No-Mite!" Interview

REMEMBER THAT YOU HAVE an excellent reason for agreeing to the interview. That reason will always be an opportunity to deliver at least two or three key points about your company or product to the audiences likely to read, see, or hear your interview.

Keep Shooting for the Basket

Always get your key messages out first. Then get them out second, third, and fourth. It's like repeat basketball: Step up to the basket, and just keep trying for that shot. And never miss those messaging opportunities, even if you have to write them on your hand. You may sound repetitive, but actually, the restatements often clarify the angle for the reporter, who may even appreciate your highlighting the most important ideas. What's more, if you wait for the reporter to ask you the right question, you may never get the chance.

However, driving home those messages doesn't mean hitting the repeat button for ten minutes. Think of key messages as *themes* rather than scripts for memorization. Verbatim regurgitation will make you sound stilted and erode your credibility, especially if your main points are in every answer. Don't be afraid of variety as long as you are expressing your key themes consistently.

Also, always be alert for the opportunities presented by the general questions at the start of an interview, as well as the "anything else?" variety at the end. For example, in the spring of 2002, I appeared on the *Today* show with Katie Couric to talk about my then-newest book. I showed off newfangled robots, mobile phones that doubled as movie theatres, and even a printed swatch that you could taste!

But the book wasn't just about the latest in circuitry; it was also about the larger trends shaping our world in the future. Katie's "anything else" question provided an opening for me to make that point, letting the viewers get a more complete idea of what the book is about. That day, its sales rank on Amazon.com jumped considerably, proving I maximized my media opportunity.

You should clearly articulate your key messages in your mind. Write them down, e-mail them to yourself, or sing them in the shower. Do whatever it takes for you to remember them best. Before you begin an interview, think about how to present them in terms that your intended audiences will understand. Audiences will vary, depending on the interview and the media outlet, and although the media itself often can be considered an audience (you want other journalists who are watching or reading to pick up the story, too!), the reporter you're talking to is not really your target. The deep-pocketed viewing public is. Think of the reporter as an information conduit, and know how you want to use that conduit before the interview begins.

Exercise Your Rights

In fact, protest for the information you need to prepare properly. Even if you have to hold up a sign! In other words, don't be shy about asking a reporter for information on the subject of the story, who else has been interviewed, and so on. You may not get a complete answer, but you do have every right to ask. In any case, taking the lead by asking questions helps set the pace and establish control at the outset. Remaining cordial and professional with the reporter is the key.

Along the same lines, don't hesitate to set ground rules as part of your initial queries. For example, you may want to stake out the areas you can and can't address by establishing your credentials and expertise at the outset of an interview. Peter Guber, Hollywood producer and chief of Mandalay Entertainment, cowrote a book, *Shoot Out: Surviving Fame and Misfortune in Hollywood,* a guide to how and why movies are made for all those trying to crack the tinsel-town code.

Peter was also the former honcho at Sony Entertainment, where he cut a billion-dollar deal to leave the studio's helm. Of course, everyone in the media wanted details of the deal. But Peter wasn't there to tell his Sony story; he was there to sell his book. He let inquiring journalists know right off the bat that the Sony conversation was off limits and that if they wanted to talk, it would be about the book and nothing else. His honest, up-front approach made for smooth interviews and great reviews.

Keep It All Business

Always remain professionally cordial during the interview, no matter how warm and friendly a reporter may be. That is, stay upbeat and cooperative, but don't let your guard down during an interview that appears to be going smoothly and easily. Such a mental lapse sets you up to be caught off guard by a tough question and can lull you away from your goal of communicating directly to your audience. Eat lightly and have a cup of coffee if you need a lift. Perhaps you could even try to schedule the interview at a place where you have "special" meetings. In general, the less the interview is like every other meeting you have, the better.

Be Enthusiastic

If you are not "up" for the interview, or do not seem to be excited about your topic, the audience will not be interested either. Even in print, enthusiasm shows. Faking it in this case is more than acceptable—it's a must. Think of it as the first time you're meeting your future spouse's parents. Work really hard to be upbeat and sell all the great things you've done, so everyone can buy into your story. But don't seem too fake, and don't be a bore. Wear a sincere, unforced smile, show interest, and act engaged in the conversation.

Relax

That's the best thing you can do. Remember, you're the one with the experience and the answers, so you own the interview—no one else. As with a skilled golf swing, you have to concentrate on a dozen different things—head up, arm straight, and so on. At the same time, you need to stay relaxed to generate booming power. But rest assured that speaking naturally, the same way you do with family and friends, is the best way to handle a media interview. Reporters need you as much as you need them. You and your product are credible enough to warrant the interview in the first place. Don't forget that you are the expert. Seriously—relax! That's it.

Recognize Your Responsibilities

Tell the truth. Don't exaggerate. Don't speculate. Don't speculate. Don't speculate. (Repeated for a reason.) Making things up even for a split second will create royal headaches for you. Therefore, if you don't know something, say so. If you can, promise to find out. If you promise to find out, do it—and as fast as possible. It builds credibility as well as creating another opportunity to talk about your company or product.

Here's why you shouldn't make things up. In the wake of September 11, some companies thought (wrongly) that there might be some marketing opportunities up for grabs. One such company was Steve Madden, Ltd. The maker of chunky, trendy shoes created a sneaker with the Stars and Stripes beaded into the side and told everyone in earshot that it was giving the proceeds to New York's recovery fund. A few probing journalists quickly found out that the donations were not being made and publicized that fact. Needless to say, no one bought the sneakers, and they were pulled from the shelves.

Don't Dribble Out Bad News

If you have bad news to report, get it out of the way all at once. It's okay. Things get better. This doesn't mean that you have to talk about it at every opportunity, but if the reporter's questioning is following that path, don't try to hide it, because the reporter knows anyway. The trick is to put the bad news into perspective. Don't let journalists give the impression that the news is really bigger than it is.

And don't be afraid of silence. Pithy, confident answers are best. The more you talk, the more your great message is lost in the mix. If you have something powerful to say, put it out there and let it bask in golden silence.

Neutralize Difficult Questions by Bridging

Along with flagging (below), bridging is the most important skill to have when you are being interviewed. These are transitional phrases that will get you out of trouble and onto safer ground. Bridging phrases might include:

- ❏ "That's an interesting question, but what you really need to focus on is …"
- ❏ "Well, the answer is no, but what is really important here is …"
- ❏ "Did you know that …"
- ❏ "What we mustn't lose sight of is …"
- ❏ "Let me answer by putting things into context."
- ❏ "You have no idea what you're talking about …." (Forget this last one, even if it's what you're really thinking.)

Flagging Ideas for the Audience to Take Away

Indicating what should be remembered is one of the most important things you can do during the interview. Flagging basically means hanging a verbal exclamation mark on the message you just delivered. Sometimes a writer doesn't understand what you're trying to explain, or doesn't see the importance in your message. She's stopped taking notes, and you've lost her. We call that film and glaze—when a film coats the face and a glaze appears in her eyes.

By flagging and *not nagging* appropriately, you can get their pens going again and reignite interest. Like with bridging, any phrase can be a flag: "What's most important is ... ," "I can't stress enough the importance of ... ," "We've sold a zillion widgets because... ," and our favorite, "You should write this down." On their own, flagging statements sound unimportant and silly, but in the context of an interview, they're crucial, albeit sometimes difficult to do just right.

Another great way to use this technique is to have a special closing version of your key messages clearly mapped out, in a way that signals their importance. It should be something that is ready to use at any time. Here are some good flagging phrases to use in your closing words or at any point in the interview:

❑ "I'd just like to reiterate ..."
❑ "Finally, the most important thing people need to know is ..."
❑ "There are three things to highlight at this point ..."

or, obvious but effective ...

❑ "This is important!"
❑ "Excuse me!" (or, "Hey! Wait a minute here!") "I was talking" (only applicable to the rudest interviewers).

Tips for Staying Out of Harm's Way

OKAY. YOU KNOW HOW TO BRIDGE, and you know you've got to hoist a flag to let interviewers know what's important. You have an agenda, and you're focused on making the conversation yours.

But you're not done. During the interview, you need to make sure you stay out of harm's way, both in what you say and how you say it. How do you get into trouble? Let us count the ways ...

Don't Answer Mechanically

An interview is not a deposition. It is your forum for getting your key messages across. On the other hand, don't let yourself get distracted for the sake of being entertaining. To that end, always think your answers through. For your first few interviews, grab a friend or coworker who knows something about your business or big idea and let her interview you. Take note of the answers you gave that you weren't happy with, and take the time to make them better by bridging back to your message. During the actual interview, feel free to rephrase or clarify your initial statement. Always go to the mat to correct an inaccurate statement. If a reporter interrupts you, listen patiently to the interjected question, acknowledge that you will answer it, and then resume making your original point. This is your time. And, as Fran Lebowitz once aptly explained, "The opposite of talking is waiting." This is especially so in interviews.

Make Your Delivery Anecdotal and Conversational

Use stories and analogies to emphasize or clarify your statements. On the other hand, be careful of humor. While it can be useful, it can also backfire. We have found that too much comedy is a bane to the existence of any serious reporter and can get a less serious reporter totally off track. So unless you are, in fact, the next Henny Youngman, lay off the funny stuff. Until later, after the piece is prepared, finished, and out the door.

Don't Stray into the "No Comment" Minefield

We've said it before and we'll say it again: If you don't want to answer a question, *do not* say, "No comment." That is just bogus. You have a comment—you just don't want to share it with the person in front of you. Instead of "No comment," answer the *durn* question as best as you can and move on, or explain why you cannot answer. Be polite. Avoid diverting the focus of the interview from your key messages! Ever.

Don't Assume Audience Knowledge of Your Industry

Don't use industry jargon or words and names unique to your professional community, because even if the reporter understands them, your audience may not. (Chances are the reporter knows half of what you're saying. Trust us.) Jargon is awful to many people's ears. That is one reason why you must immediately rid yourself of it. Sounding like a trade magazine is deadly for any interview. Use plain English.

Don't Answer Hypothetical Questions

You're there to talk about the real world. Reporters usually ask hypothetical questions to get your reaction to a sticky situation. Answering hypothetical questions—whether it's your boss, your spouse, or the media who's doing the asking—will always come back to haunt you. If you must answer, respond by putting the question into context with an actual event or experience.

Use Positive Words as Often as Possible

The power of the positive is especially important. A positive response is especially preferable when the alternative is a double negative. In other words, say "good" rather than "not bad." How's business? "Excellent! We just signed a deal."

More to the point, positive words can't be taken out of context and misquoted as easily. For instance, Nixon swore, "I'm not a crook!" We, of course, all knew he was as soon as he said it. Clinton didn't have sexual relations with that woman, either ... right?

Remember that perception often is reality in the media game. Therefore, always use "I" instead of "you." Deep breath: Practice in front of a mirror. "You" sounds like a pointed finger. Your friends may have told you that. Many members of your audience will take away only the flavor of your key messages; you don't want the taste that lingers to be negative. And using the word "you" can sound accusatory—or schoolmarmish. *You* want to be easygoing.

Don't Let a Reporter Put Words in Your Mouth

Don't repeat any negative or erroneous language that a reporter may use. What you say can and will be used against you outside a court of law. In all seriousness, anything you say will be attributed to you if you do not clarify your meaning for the reporter. Also, listen intently to what a reporter recites back to you. Is it what you said, or what he *thinks* you said? What's said and how it's interpreted are usually two different things. Make sure the reporter understands your answer before it's written down in tomorrow's paper, in black and scary print.

Urgent: Nothing Is off the Record

Haven't we said that already? We'll say it again! Casually agreeing to speak off the record is reckless and foolhardy. Above all, remember that whatever conditions you set, you have absolutely no control over the information once you decide to speak up.

In journalism, there is a bizarre animal called "talking for background." We have no idea who invented this—we'd like to meet and chastise that person—because the only time we counsel people to talk on background is if they *really expect to be quoted.* It's not that reporters are unethical. It's more that there is no written, or even implied, contract between the reporter and the interviewee. It's nonbinding. You'd be nuts to think otherwise.

It's Not the Clothes You Wear ...

WHEN CONTEMPLATING HOW to make a good impression, most people don't think beyond dressing appropriately and combing their hair. In fact, the way you sit, stand, and move has a lot more to do with how you come across during an interview. Therefore, be extremely conscious of body language. Your appearance is just as important as what you say. Even in print interviews that your audiences will never see, the wrong body language can divert a reporter's attention from your key messages and even signal areas you wish to avoid.

Body language should always convey energy—the sparkle that you get when you know something exciting and can't wait to share it. Energy is not New Agey. It's very real. Pay attention to the way you react to people when you talk to them. In particular, make and maintain eye contact with the interviewer. Shifting your eyes and evading direct eye contact conveys impatience, discomfort, guilt, or lack of interest. Keep your gaze slightly upward. Listen intently, and lean slightly forward if you are at a desk.

Don't drum on a table with your fingers, swivel in your chair, jingle keys in your pockets, rustle papers, or toy with microphones, pencils, water glasses, and clothing. In particular, keep your hands away from your face. In addition to betraying your uneasiness, these gestures will be amplified by broadcast equipment to distracting and embarrassing levels.

Don't nod as you listen to a negative or erroneous question. Nodding is wrong—period. The act of nodding is an involuntary response when you understand a question, and although it's quite normal, it can create some very problematic impressions. Nodding without saying anything first won't look great in any situation. But *nodding at something you are entirely against or confused by* can be interpreted as confirmation of the question. Saying "ah ha!" and "yes" and "yeah" all the time is even worse. Do it in front of a mirror and you'll see why right away. Likewise, don't smile or laugh inappropriately if a question catches you off guard. These reactions convey guilty surprise. Also, be careful about smiling to demonstrate your understanding of a question or point; the gesture could be misconstrued as smug or arrogant. If you flub an answer, ask for the opportunity to restate. "May I start again?" is acceptable. If they say no, sorry, do it anyway. Nothing ventured, nothing gained.

Finally, avoid eating a heavy meal before an interview, because digestion uses a large amount of energy and you won't be "on" 100 percent. And, if you happen to be doing phone interviews, please stand (see Chapter 5). That will make your energy rise and help you convey a positive attitude through your voice.

The Postmortem

OKAY, THE INTERVIEW IS OVER, and you lived to tell about it. But you still have some follow-up work to do. For example, once the interview is over, don't be afraid to double-check facts and quotes. E-mail or call the reporter to see if she has any other questions, whether she understood what you said, if she needs some more supporting information, and so on.

Also, stay in contact with the reporter after the initial interview. The reporter usually will not call to read her story to you. However, be sure to tell the reporter to call you without hesitation should she need any clarification or further information.

Beyond the coverage itself, the goal, as we mentioned, is to be asked back again and again. Great guests on TV news shows or stellar interviewees for publications are called again, and that's how you build buzz—through the return appearance.

You get the callback in two ways. The first is by having great answers, sticking to the message, and giving a great story. The second—after you've mastered the interview—is to be helpful and to assist the journalist with the process. (Oh, and just be nice.) Send any information you have that would be useful, connect her with other people who might be able to add to the story, and cough up some related white papers if you have them. It doesn't hurt to send a handwritten thank-you note, either. A simple "I enjoyed the experience of working with you" will do the trick.

PART III

Taking
Media
Exposure
to the Next Level

Source Filing 101

THIS CHAPTER IS ABOUT the process of meeting with journalists in a particular field, face-to-face, not to discuss your news of the moment, as often there isn't any, but to make a personal connection and demonstrate the constellation of subjects that you're qualified to speak about outside the topical confines of your business or service. And what do you get? Lots (sometimes tons) of coverage.

One of the best ways for a novice to start in media relations is by source filing himself. Source filing is more work for someone who is doing PR, but it makes life much easier in the long run. Source filing, in a nutshell, is establishing yourself as an expert and finding your way into a reporter's Rolodex, whether or not the reporter is currently working on a story that can include you. In other words, the goal is to position yourself as an authority on a variety of topics.

We have seen time and time again the value of source filing. Journalists need to know experts who are willing and available to comment on important events and developments. Once you become an established source in reporters' Rolodexes, you'll start receiving frequent calls, and then, frequent clips! The beauty of source filing is simple: You offer yourself to a journalist as a source, an expert qualified to speak to the media on one or more subjects, usually (but not always) in your industry. The journalist may not need to use your quotes right away, perhaps not even for several months, but based on the knowledge and expertise you demonstrate in an initial conversation, he files your name away for future reference.

Suppose that sometime down the road, the reporter is working on a story about your industry or other field of expertise. Looking through his list of viable contacts, he realizes that you're the perfect person to fill the hole in his story—the expert who can give the real inside scoop about the competitive environment in an industry or why some new legislation could spell disaster for smaller businesses in your region. Or suppose you have a story about your company that you want to pitch to the media. This same journalist is now somebody that you've cultivated by offering yourself as a source for him, and because you already have an established connection with him (and that's what PR is all about), the chances of your getting an opportunity to give your pitch are much better.

Source filing feeds off pitching your news, and pitching the news gets a boost from source filing. You do it before, after, and during your regular, everyday media push for success—that is, while you're out there flogging the press for news coverage. Source file everywhere and with everyone possible—on the national and local levels, with the print and the broadcast media. You never know when it's going to bear fruit for you, and when it does, the results can be tremendous.

In 1995, a Web visionary named Nicholas Butterworth wanted to publicize his company, SonicNet, a new type of music-related website. The site, run by nerdy but brilliant music aficionados, offered the first opportunity for a serious music lover to find genuinely new, little known but high-quality material on the Web—and download fantastic sounding clips, too. Nicholas had a small buzz around him already through his previous stint with Rock the Vote, something that got MTV kids voting in the pre-Clinton era.

At the time, SonicNet had no major news to report yet, but we decided to source file Nicholas. We took him around town to meet various journalists, introducing him as the person who was going to bring "coolness" to the Net. Until then, journalists had met no one involved with the Internet music scene but rock-and-roll techno dweebs. And what else? Nicholas and his cronies introduced a true business model to Internet music by relying on multiple revenue streams: online services, sales of items online, and, one day in the near future (this was 1995), revenues from paid ads on its website.

Journalists scoffed but were amused by the idea, anyway. Eventually, source filing paid off in a big way: Five months after we sourced Nicholas B., SonicNet met all three of its goals through deals with the then-famous online service Prodigy, the selling of shirts for The Cure, and ad deals with Levi's and Jägermeister. The same journalists who had been there from the beginning now knew that Nicholas was in demand, and SonicNet began getting far more media exposure and was soon able to make money for its owners.

I have established expertise with the media in several interesting ways. None of them are directly related to being a PR muckety-muck, but exposure is exposure, and that's what source filing is all about. For example, I am notorious for my addiction to e-mail, and to respond to e-mail messages within minutes (an interactive e-mail pager is his codependent device). When we discovered that *U.S. News & World Report* was doing a story about "e-mail addiction," it was a perfect opportunity to promote myself—and the business.

I described to *U.S. News* how I deal with hundreds of e-mails a day, and even drive fifteen miles to pick up my mail when my e-pager is out of range. This story did not directly relate to RLM on the surface, but, as the CEO of a PR firm, it made me look extremely conscientious and plugged in, and I made sure that RLM was prominently mentioned. (Fact-checking—or calling the reporter to go over my material—assured that my ID wasn't merely "Laermer, e-mail junkie.")

People have been source filing in one way or another for years, but too often they're not very good at it—they make it much too complicated. If you know which reporter or segment producer is right for the angle you are proposing or plan to propose (whether about you, your product, or your business), then that person needs to meet you *before* they start thinking which person might make an ideal interview for the story. You can pitch hard later, but earlier is the time for them just to get to know you. It's your job to help them understand why you are the ultimate source. Source filing, repeat after me, is the best way to get the media in on your goodness early on.

Again, Do Your Homework

OKAY, NOW YOU UNDERSTAND why source filing is a vital part of your media strategy. How do you begin? You might be surprised to learn that you shouldn't cover the waterfront. Be choosy. Rather than send out releases en masse, target individuals drawn from your research. These are contacts that you can tell will be especially interested in the story. Use your gut. Think about the story you're reading—is that reporter interested in you or your product? Or even in some offbeat fact or tangent that you can then tie in to your product?

The strategy of *doing your homework* is worthwhile because effective matchmaking works. As a source, you must have valid, newsworthy information, or you shouldn't waste a reporter's time. However, you must always remember that newsworthiness is indubitably subjective. A story that's interesting to a reporter at *Fortune* may not be fascinating to the editorial staff at *The Economist,* and vice versa. Something that's perfect for your home paper might be bad news, so to speak, for the local bureau of a national magazine. That whole idea of showering releases (even source filing information) on journalists everywhere, without taking the time to think about what that person writes about and how your story will help him, will get you in trouble—every time. So always be judicious about whom you contact. Think.

Targeting the right journalists with whom to source file yourself isn't as enormous a task as it might appear. Most media relations professionals spend a lot of time creating contact lists, because it's common wisdom that this is the best way to target the media. While lists can be a good idea for other approaches, with source filing, it's usually best to do your homework with the newspaper at your side. The Internet is your secondary companion here, because once you've found a likely prospect in the newspaper, you can always use the Internet to check the stories a reporter has done in the past, as well as read the entire text of his articles. And then you will know for sure if that reporter is yours for the taking.

Let's look at a few examples of how the right context can really make things happen for you, media-wise. We know a modern dancer who had become a choreographer. She was starting her own dance company, which takes *chutzpah* even in an economic upturn. Martha wanted a critic at the *New York Times* to get to know her and the newfangled dance turns she was creating. But Martha was sure this was unacceptable behavior—until we cajoled her into phoning. It turned out the critic she was enamored with had a real interest in the type of work she was doing.

With Buzz Abuzz, Somebody's Bound to Get Stung

Solution(s), robust, turnkey, interactive, best of breed, scalable, next-generation, Web-enabled, seamless, end-to-end.

What do all these words have in common? They have no meaning outside of the culture (culcha) of hype. They're all part of a list of "buzzwords and phrases we could do without," according to the people at www.buzzkiller.net. The Buzz Saw, as it's known, is a website on a mission to educate all English-speaking people about these nonwords in an attempt to create a grassroots revolution against them.

Caroline Waxler, a journalist and cofounder of the site, explains where these words were born. "Our whole language has become much more casual. We've started to sum down* everything to one word— e-this, i-that." The idea behind using jargon, she continued, "is that you use big words to connote a certain authority and expertise. People want to appear cutting edge. If they use these 'cutting edge' words, a reporter who doesn't know the term may get intrigued."

She got press—not for the show she was working on at the time, but the next one. The idea here was Martha got "in" with her favorite critic, with one cup of coffee that paid off in spades later.

In the winter of 2002, one of the best media consultants and speech trainers we know, named Ginny Pulos, was suffering through the horrors of a no-business period. We tried to get her to talk about her experiences working with high-level CEOs for, among others, *Chief Executive* magazine—that is, to source file her own fabulous work. We wanted her to talk with *CE* about her work with CEOs. She was someone who could teach a chief executive to have real confidence about public speaking. And few did it with as much verve and aplomb as she, or so her fans thought.

But Ginny said she found it difficult, if not downright impossible, to ask the CEOs to reveal that she was indeed helping them with such leadership goals. To which we responded, "Find

And that's where a beginner in PR will trip up, every time. Good PR people are precise. Much of the friction between PR pros and journalists comes from the indiscriminate, mass pitching that less experienced or less enlightened professionals disseminate. Throw buzzwords in, and the problem doubles or triples. When you're contacting journalists and trying to cultivate relationships with them, you have to talk like real people, and you have to talk fast because they are busy (aren't we all?).

Final word on the horrible habit of using cruddy, meaningless phrases, words, and coinages: It's a war without frontiers out there, and the boundaries begin with you. Therefore, before you source file yourself or pitch a story to a reporter, producer, or anyone else in the media, rout out the jargon first. You'll get the best results by using honest, plain English. It's your language; don't bastardize it.

*Let's remember that journalists aren't immune to this plague, either.

someone who'll talk on the record. This is what you need to do! When you want PR, contact your own clients and call in a favor. Plus, you're giving them their own shot at publicity in a national magazine." She took our advice and was eventually featured in a magazine that wanted to see how she did that voodoo that she did so well (here's to you, Cole Porter).

Here she was, keeping the connections with media going during lean times. See, at the time, she had nothing to say, as it were, that was newsworthy or even topical ... but she found a way to get into a reporter's file expediently. As anyone who's been around can tell you, during highly profitable times you don't ask your clients to help you with stories: Why would you risk it or waste the time? It's during the tough times that you ask the favors. People at the top have been doing it for years. This is part of the reason why they're there.

Source filing is like a time-delayed pitch. You are the expert, and the media needs to know you. You can always call a reporter later with a news angle for a time-sensitive story, but they aren't going to call you unless they *know* you. And knowing you and what you can do for their story is what it's all about.

Get This Party Started

WHEN YOU'RE SEARCHING for the right journalists with whom to source yourself, leave no stone unturned. And think about your industry—hard. You might want to go after the so-called trade magazines and newsletters. Hit the generational press—if it's a product for a younger market, go to generation X, Y, or Z magazines. If it's a garden product, you can source yourself as a horticulture expert. And don't rule out the alternative media. Those biweekly and weekly "rags" are often free, but nevertheless they're places where people get their news, and yours might be just the mini profile article that these folks are looking for.

The Initial Mailing

Start with an intro mailing that has basic information—and perhaps something of "new" interest to the reporter. If you're already somewhat known in a field, then you want to make sure that trade or industry publications are kept abreast of the latest accomplishments under your well-armed belt. Do you have awards? Famous clients? You have a product that's received a mention in a magazine? Got a famous dad or partner? Have you discovered something new about the field that this reporter should immediately be made aware of? These are the facts that trade publications want to know. And by trade publications, we also should consider what's on the Internet: Use Google.com to search under "X industry trade magazines" and "X industry online magazines" (almost always trades).

Here's what you will need to put into your media mailings, regardless of your fame quotient. With these mailings (mostly online or e-mail in this day and age) include the following coolly developed items, handily attached:

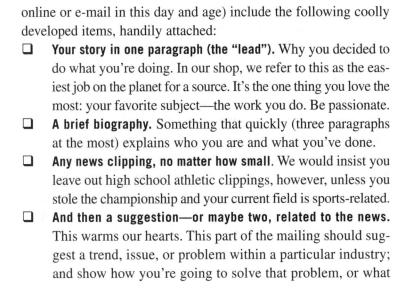

- ❑ **Your story in one paragraph (the "lead").** Why you decided to do what you're doing. In our shop, we refer to this as the easiest job on the planet for a source. It's the one thing you love the most: your favorite subject—the work you do. Be passionate.
- ❑ **A brief biography.** Something that quickly (three paragraphs at the most) explains who you are and what you've done.
- ❑ **Any news clipping, no matter how small.** We would insist you leave out high school athletic clippings, however, unless you stole the championship and your current field is sports-related.
- ❑ **And then a suggestion—or maybe two, related to the news.** This warms our hearts. This part of the mailing should suggest a trend, issue, or problem within a particular industry; and show how you're going to solve that problem, or what you can say about the trend.

Do not make this document formal. Many people think it's important to follow a standard formula for such mailings, but formula writing is not the way to get attention. The stiffest letters are the easiest to ignore; you read—and ultimately respond to—the ones that make you think, smile, or perhaps chuckle. Get the words out fast, in the lead, and go for the gusto. Time and time again we tell people: You are writing about the subject you love the most, besides your life partner or goldfish. Just spew it out, passionately. And then edit the heck out of it! Mark Twain said, "If I had had more time, I'd have written less." He knew what he was talking about.

Examples of prime announcement subjects are partnerships, new product debuts, new executive hires, new office locations, and so on. But don't engage in arbitrary mailings. Target. Don't blanket. In other words, if you throw every piece of news at reporters, they won't be interested in anything you have to say. Also, try to include a news peg—that is, a date on which the news is breaking. This minimizes a reporter's tendency to procrastinate and sit on the story as if it were a dinosaur egg. Of course, you could tell the reporter that someone else will run the story on day X, but that is, of course, the last resort. It's a negotiating tool.

The Mechanics of Follow-Up

After you've sent out your mailing, follow it up with a phone call a few days to a week later. We once did a press event for a major satellite company launching its first high-speed effort in Washington, D.C. We managed to get fifty reporters to come to this morning event and actually cover it on the day before the oddest Presidential election in history. Months later, we were meeting with a software firm in Seattle (not Microsoft, thanks) and they read our case study of the event. They asked us, "How did you get so many folks to show up?" The simple reply: "We called them." So don't forget to call.

After you've done the initial mailing and your follow-up phone call, wait. Because if the source filing works, and it will, you will get return phone calls before you expect them to start. But please don't leave voice mails. In the media relations business, that's as good as not calling. Do not sound desperate. Just explain your angle as simply as possible, so that the reporter or producer realizes that she "has a shot" at something. If you're telling the truth, she'll bite. And, if you are at your wit's end and can't get her, hit zero when the voice-mail system picks up, get through to an operator and ask when the journalist will be there. Then call her at the prescribed time.

After that, with luck, a meeting ensues—perhaps even one on the phone. Don't be disappointed if the journalist has only enough time for a phone call. You can accomplish a lot on the phone if you pretend the meeting is in person. Have an agenda handy (although you may want to keep that to yourself), get through your points, and get off the phone, so you can let the journalist reflect on how fascinating you and your company are.

After you've had that friendly call, let's talk about furthering your source filing. How about a small piece of mail—anything, really, that explains what you do, on a postcard, but one that looks awesome? Don't forget that no matter how good your product is, you only have a fraction of a second to register its existence with today's media-saturated consumer.

Or perhaps you need to find something with which to source file yourself, something that demonstrates what you do so well. For example, in 1995 Tower Air, a low-cost airline in New York, came to us when it ran into some image problems in the media after its baggage handlers lost passengers' pets three times in a row. Our job was to get the media to stop giving them a hard time for, well, losing pets. The passengers eventually got their pets back, but the media referred to them as the airline that lost pets, and that is not exactly the image you want to convey to American families.

So Tower enacted Pets Fly Free Day. This was a day in April when anybody who flew with Tower could fly their pets for free. Tower received a ton of press and press *acclaim,* and in general, a lot of buzz in the tri-state area. Source filing was a nice way to get people to stop talking about the negatives and to start looking at Tower more positively. What Tower did was to put out a message that said, essentially, "We recognize that we have a procedural problem with the handling of pets and we are fixing it. And in the meantime, we are trying to make amends for the inconveniences people have suffered."

About two months later, at a Tower board meeting, there emerged an unusual and serendipitous angle: Tower traveled to the Middle East every day, but in that time period, it had had to severely curtail its flight schedule because of Ramadan, the month of fasting and reflection for thousands of Muslims in that region of the world. It occurred to us that this might have been the only airline in history to change its schedule based on the *lunar calendar.* This bit of information was leaked to the *Wall Street Journal,* which saw it as a first for airlines, and suddenly Tower had taken another important step in source filing itself with the media.

Doing the Two-Step

LET'S LOOK AT SUCCESSFUL two-step source filing, another technique you may want to consider. The FeedRoom, a very unusual high-speed technology company, was launched in 1999. Amidst a huddle of narrow-band news sites, The FeedRoom had a unique approach to broadband, as well as its team of broadcast news veterans. The FeedRoom proposed aggregating video "feeds" from leading networks, local TV and radio stations, cable channels, program producers, and print sources, and placing all of them into a consumer-friendly, easy-to-find location on the Web.

At its inception, The FeedRoom had to overcome rumors that "broadband isn't here yet," and that it had yet to sign partnerships of note. Also, the company was just a month old and had no customers or finished technology. Yet, it was determined not to be another "dumb" dot-com.

Step One, Step Two

To fuel expansion and ensure survival, the source filing methodology highlighted not The FeedRoom but Jonathan Klein, its founder, former executive VP at CBS News and an originator of *48 Hrs.* He wanted people "in the know" to realize that he was out of TV, forever. That in itself was interesting enough to create a storm of interest in meeting him. But as a source, Klein also needed a more enticing angle to really rev up interest in The FeedRoom.

Klein wanted to talk to the media about the future, and do this without seeming as if he didn't have a product! The solution was not a news story but a concept to shop around to the media. The concept was that one person—a TV veteran—can "own" the broadband news space by creating a first interactive, broadband television news network and by providing personalized rich-media (a form of online-accessible text) newscasts to Internet users through a website and affiliated partners. The concept was crystallized in this intriguing trademark: TV 2.0.

In an effort to show its faith in this brand-new broadband medium (remember, this was 1999), and to distinguish the company as a true leader in the rich-media news arena, The FeedRoom sent out a letter spinning out this concept to a select group of journalists. One week later, The FeedRoom followed that up with an actual broadband-accessible video press release to announce the first two Klein partnerships. The notion was to take what Klein had—broadband itself—and bring it to the press, who already were familiar with him by virtue of the prior letter.

The press release contained The FeedRoom's major partnership with NBC Interactive, a part of the media giant NBC (and the Tribune Company, another major broadcaster). This webcast was easy to access for anyone who had a decent Web connection. The final product consisted of all three representatives—FeedRoom's, NBC's, and NBC Interactive's—speaking about the value of The FeedRoom to their news organizations, surrounded by interactive links to other press releases and information.

One day before the release, the same reporters who had been sent the original source filing memo were alerted to watch their e-mail boxes. The following day, an e-mail message with a link to The FeedRoom site and the video release was sent to them. These journalists were then able to see the power of video, broadband, and The FeedRoom for themselves, and no one was unwilling to give Klein a few minutes to learn his whole story.

The following month Klein was featured in a number of publications, including the *New York Times,* CNNfn, *Chicago Tribune, Broadcasting & Cable, Forbes, Electronic Media,* and several others. That was followed by additional coverage in the Associated Press, *Advertising Age Global, PRWeek, AdWeek,* News.com, *San Jose Business Journal,* and *Wired.* From this initial source filing effort, The FeedRoom was then able to develop its leadership position in the broadband news industry. Journalists began calling more frequently for follow-up stories on TV2.0.

An Alternative Scenario

What about something simple—without a high-profile character as the source filer? Let's take New York–based startup Social Science as an example. When Social Science's group of five twenty-six year olds (yes, they were all twenty-six) came to RLM to sort out the release of Net Discussion, a gorgeous but difficult-to-explain chat software, we knew that this was going to be very tough. The people behind the newfound technology were, well, really green. They were a bunch of guys who'd been in graduate school together and were aiming to become the next great software producers in New York.

Naturally, it was essential to sit down with the creators and marketers and ensure that they were forthright and totally realistic about whom they were trying to partner with and what their guarantees were. The reason for all this soul-searching was that reporters would need to be assured that Social Science was not just another company that would go up in smoke in five minutes. It was also important to discuss the competition—rich, to say the least—and of course, real numbers: the cost of the software; the upgrade fee; and especially, since they were selling to corporations, the maintenance cost.

Once we were satisfied that the group had a viable product, we decided to source file them as "rock stars," even though they weren't. In the '60s and '70s, kids left school to become rock singers or guitarists; in the late '90s, they left school to become producers in the new media world.

Media players immediately understood the message—the idea was that in the early Net days, these guys were getting together not to be rock stars but real Net players. That worked well as a media metaphor in the heady Internet days of the late '90s. And since the founders of Social Science were smart and able to communicate the well-honed message, an interview with them was easy to parlay into success.

Net Discussion set up a special URL for reporters, allowing them to try the chat software. By the way, setting up a special URL is easy—*and* it makes you look like a heart surgeon. Take the Internet address you currently have and add a "/media" to it. Add one page of easy HTML, which the press can use to gather information, and voilà! You've established your Net-savvy credentials.

Social Science also created several key partnerships with local companies, particularly in the media arena that we knew the press loved to sink their keyboards into. Reporters and, notably, some high-level local TV producers began clamoring to meet a tiny software group in Manhattan's Lower West Side that put out good-looking chat software while working with some of the top software developers in their crowded field. Their quotes started appearing in Forbes.com, the *New York Post,* the *New York Observer,* and *eWeek,* which described the twenty-somethings as a team working to develop a useful product for all new media companies.

After two months of sourcing them around New York as rock stars to the business world, we stopped using the rock star angle. Eventually Social Science simply became known as the easier, cheaper alternative to popular Net accessory I-Chat and other softwares that were hard to install, expensive, and standard (read cliché).

The founders of Social Science eventually nailed an interview with the editor of the *Wall Street Journal* "Under The Radar" column. The *Journal* gave them a thumbs-up in a story, describing them as a company that was putting "all their chips" into the Web world. In its first few months, Social Science (soon known as Site Bridge) had learned how to develop its new product purely for financial sites to use—and pay for. This was a new tack, and as such it garnered a plethora of press.

It's Not All about You

Our parents' idea of success was to land a job with a great company. It didn't matter what job, as long as it was in the right building. Success came from working for IBM or Western Electric or wherever for the long haul, climbing your way through the ranks and making a name for yourself within its halls.

During the past decade (give or take a few years), that formula for achievement bit the dust. Thanks to a hyperactive market, short-lived businesses, and experimentation, people don't stay in the same place for very long. In the mid to late '90s, executives (and everyone who thought they could be) began courting the media in ways never seen before. The idea was to build a clip book not only for your business or product, but for yourself as well. There was plenty of money to be spent on talent, and every start-up wanted the hottest Web designer, CFO, COO, CMO, and CEO. Workers were hell-bent on creating demand for their talents, know-

Make Yourself Accessible

If you remember nothing else about source filing, remember this: access. By that we mean that you must make yourself accessible to the press once you've set the source filing wheels in motion. If you are constantly unavailable, you send out several messages, all of them negative: that you're not interested, that you don't take the press seriously, that you don't want to play the game, or that you're not the real thing. It's a simple equation: Any one of these "nots" equals "no press coverage." This is where you have to be careful, because once you burn the media, you rarely get a second chance at source filing.

We worked with a company we'll call Clic Vu during the dot-com heyday. Nearly every entrepreneur can get mired in the idea that he or his product is the greatest thing ever, but the founders of Clic Vu suffered from an extreme case of self-

ing the next job was just a phone call away. And how!

Once the market took the deep dive, the "cult of personality" went buh-bye. Guys like Bill Gross of Idealab, who went through great pains to become household names, soon were the notorious poster boys of the Web's demise. The previous publicity frenzy was a bad use of the media. It was never real news, and being in the spotlight ultimately proved to be hazardous to professional health.

Thankfully, a smarter, more experienced PR market approach emerged from the lesson of the '90s, and you should always keep that in mind when you're source filing yourself. The concept of plain self-promotion has evaporated. Smart business people and entrepreneurs aren't promoting themselves anymore; they're using the media to create a profile and thus a market for their services. Demand is no longer centered principally on name recognition. Instead, it's steeped in new types of services and insight. Building media awareness about your business, rather than yourself, is the new way to drive deals.

importance. Our source filing expedition led to a phone interview with *iMarketing News,* which was the most influential trade publication for Clic Vu. One founder insisted that he and his fellow founder both be on the call, but once the call started, the reporter noticed that the voices and the responses sounded too much alike. Here's what ensued:

> REPORTER (NICE GUY): "Okay. I'll tell you what. I'd like to hear from only one of you."

> COFOUNDER #1: "Let me tell you how it's done."

> REPORTER: "I've got to go now. Thanks."

Immediate Impact Zone

The following dialogue took place between Richard Laermer and saxophonist David Sanborn in 1987. Keep it in mind when you're considering the best ways to source yourself in the media.

LAERMER: *So I see you everywhere, David.*

SANBORN: *You do? How's that?*

LAERMER: *Every time there's a jam session, there you are with your interlude, jamming along or playing as soloist.*

SANBORN: *Nah. Not true. I only do about two appearances a year.*

LAERMER: *Then why do I think I'm seeing you everywhere?*

SANBORN: *Because I am very selective about taking only the highest-profile gigs. Otherwise, why bother?*

LAERMER: *Sensible.*

SANBORN: *No other way to be, man.*

Maximum impact, minimum effort. No other way to be.

The bottom line: It won't work if you think that you have all the answers. Reporters have a job to do. Help them out. In other words, make it easy for you by making it simple for them. Before you know it, you'll become the source you always knew you could be.

CHAPTER 8

Going National

YOU'VE DONE IT. You've found your angle, zeroed in on the right journalist, marked the clock, and made the right pitch at the right time. Now every newsstand, grocery store, and paperboy in the Bay Area is selling your story in the *San Francisco Examiner.* Great news, good work, bravo! With the paper's circulation inching toward the million-a-day mark, you've got a lot of potential customers reading your story that day.

But you can't rest yet. In fact, you're in danger of becoming a has-been right now! The media game is all about momentum, so you'd better keep it going, or it's sure going to evaporate fast. Every day the newspaper is filled with unique, entertaining, and newsworthy articles, and two-thirds of them end there. So move on ... fast.

Those Who Hesitate Are Lost

Our media has attention deficit disorder. Like the rest of America, it remembers only the last thing out of Paula Zahn's mouth—and because of our national ADD, everything else is a giant yawn.

The point is that when something comes along in the media that relates to what you do or what you're about as a company, don't sit around. Pounce on it, because if you haven't made the story your story within a few hours, producers will simply hang up mid-sentence when you try to get their attention.

Today's TV, radio, and print news is 24/7, not to mention pagers, phones, and the Web—you name it—also serving as news gatherers. In an average day, thousands of stories that pose as news pass our eyes, but we remember only a couple because someone gave them life past the first headline. The media's a machine, and you need to crank the media up to the highest level!

Because there are so many different types of media competing for the public's attention, you need to catapult the one news story that relates to you or your product right out of the airwaves, put your mark on it, and send it out there for the rest of the world to grab

Once you've gained some coverage in your local press, you're well on your way to creating buzz for your product. But now you have to take it to the next level. The way to get great coverage nationally is to take the exposure you receive in your local newspapers and sell it to the rest of the media nationwide.

Sound hard? It gets easier after the first time. But first, let's bask in the sunshine of good press coverage for a moment. Go to the local newsstand and pick up ten copies—at least—of the paper! Your Mom will want a clip of you to show off to her mah-jongg buddies, and so will your Aunt Elizabeth for her bridge partner. Then there's the copy you have to mail to your sister, and so on.

quickly. If your local paper reports something about your industry or about the need, say, for a product just like yours, clip the original, add a quick annotation about your company and products, plus your basic expertise, and send it to the nation's wires, reporters, editors, and columnists before the clock strikes noon.

Take advantage, too, of the fact that different media fuel each other. These days, a story in the paper was usually born from a missive online, be it an e-mail report or a wire-service tip fed to AM news shows. TV broadcasters scour the morning papers and overnight online reporting to see what they're going to report on. In turn, TV headlines translate into drive-time radio babble, the morning shows beget the noon news, and so on.

Therefore, if you see something in the morning that you can make an opportunistic yet crucial comment about, pitch yourself as the expert to every TV station around. Without an expert to add knowledge or insight on a topic, TV producers will pretty much skip on to the next story. Making yourself available (quickly!) will give the story—and you—a new and hopefully energizing life with the media.

Yes, the window is indeed small, but if you see the opportunity and seize it, coverage will come your way. Coverage is the thing we crave.

Four copies are for you. One copy belongs on the first page of your clip book—*you do have a clip book, right?* These are very important for keeping a record of your press coverage both for yourself and for customers, potential partners, and other important people. If you don't have a clip book, that's easy to rectify. Go to a local art supply store and buy a giant loose-leaf binder and a three-hole punch, plus some plastic page sleeves to keep everything looking good, or at least to prevent the clips from yellowing. You can also have the clips professionally mounted, which makes for a nicer presentation, but it certainly isn't necessary.

Getting back to your newspaper copies, you should keep the second of the four copies in your files. The last two copies should be very carefully cut and mounted with the front-page banner of the newspaper for years of photographic reproduction. You're going to need those crisp copies of your coverage to get more press and more business. Clips get damaged and disappear incredibly fast, so keep them somewhere safe, and always retain a few extras—someplace where you can find them again. That sounds simplistic, but you'd be amazed at how many people leave out that basic step, and they're always dismayed when they can't show potential new customers that they've received two years' worth of great press.

It's true, as we've said, that the immediate buzz from the story is ephemeral, but remember that media coverage is still important and useful for a long time after the print date. If you maintain good copies of your press coverage, you can use them to get much more mileage out of that *Examiner* story. So get that clip book going!

The Momentum at Hand

NOW THAT YOU'VE BASKED in your fifteen minutes of fame (and yes, why not?), it's time to get back to the momentum at hand. This is the most important part of media relations. Turning one piece of coverage into a small national phenomenon is a real skill. To do it like a pro, think fast, think tactical, and try to spot all the trends swirling around you.

You can start ramping up your coverage by getting some more local groundswell so that your story doesn't make you a one-hit wonder. Let's walk through a typical scenario so you can see how it's done. In today's *San Francisco Examiner,* on page seven, is a glowing story about a local sporting goods store—your sporting goods store. Featured is the new hybrid skateboard you and your coworkers have created. It uses a sophisticated suspension and axle system borrowed from a luxury car company to create the ultimate skateboard—the "Street Coupe." At $400, it isn't child's play, but it is revolutionizing transportation for the locals who have the dollars and the thirst for something different.

As we said, we're in the momentum business now. Momentum is a little more sophisticated than speed. Speed is simply doing something fast. Momentum gains strength as it chugs along and makes a healthy impact when it finally gets to wherever it's going. You've got to evaluate the landscape quickly to give impetus to your Street Coupe story. To do so, you keep it local at first, saturating the town in any way possible, to make sure that now everyone in the city knows that the best way to part with $400 is to ... get the Coupe. But you need to alert the national media and "the suits" that you're running a business that's worth watching. That's the first milestone in building strength and creating PR momentum—and national buzz.

When it comes to local press, big splashes can be done on the cheap. Perhaps there's a local skate park that you can commandeer for the afternoon. Bring a truckload of Street Coupes, hand them out to the kids, let them test the ride out, and, of course, invite your local TV station to give your invention a whirl, too. The ability to film a gaggle of unbiased kids ready and willing to say just how good—or bad—the ride was is a bonus for any camera crew.

But you need to plan ahead, because you should follow up any outdoor shenanigans with a local press tour and product briefing with all the local reporters. In this case, you'd need to zero in on technology, sports, automotive (the suspension and axle angle), and entertainment writers. That would help you maximize any PR possibilities you have in your favor.

If you don't have a park or some other logical location at your disposal, choose an empty parking lot close to your local newspaper or broadcast center. Of course, proximity doesn't equal coverage, but it doesn't hurt to make it easier. Make sure that all the planning directors, writers, and producers know exactly what you will be doing, and where and when. A demo model of your skateboard for their own riding pleasure wouldn't hurt, either.

Now, you've already had your first taste of press coverage with the *Examiner* story. Let's consider the rest of the print landscape. The other big paper in town is the *San Francisco Chronicle.* But the *Chronicle* isn't going to be interested in running a story their competitor printed a day earlier. As a matter of fact, it's pointless for them. What's more, a pitch to the *Chronicle* will earn you little more than a journalist disliking you and wondering if you think he's an idiot.

Okay, what about the other local papers? There's the *San Francisco Weekly, San Francisco Business Journal,* and so many others—the *Bay Guardian* even—but they all go to press once a week, and we don't have time to let our news cool off. Regional newspapers will pick it up eventually, and local newspapers will always be able to track down news that's, well, local. Let them find you, in this case.

Option number two is the big time: namely, a TV broadcast. Broadcast is important for many reasons, and here is reason number one: Newspapers don't consider broadcast news to be a competitor. In fact, the daily local news shows rely on the day's papers for the source of their reporting. And the converse is true, too—producers spend the wee hours of the morning scanning the local press to see which stories would make good visuals for a segment. Odds are that if you made it to the *San Francisco Examiner* or any local paper, the news desk at your local broadcast channel has already read your story. They're not going to say "Who?" when you call.

But the key to converting your story from the printer to the airwaves is making it look good. A camera crew isn't going to shoot your assembly line—or you, for that matter, a talking head with some bright idea. What they will shoot is something interesting to look at, a "thing" that gives viewers more information about the idea or product that can't be seen on a gray page of newsprint. The Street Coupe has visual appeal and won't take too much creative packaging for the press.

Serve It Hot

THERE ARE DOZENS of news shows in San Francisco, which is the fifth-largest media hub in the United States, so you have plenty of options. But which types of news programs are the best fit and the smartest way to gain real momentum? Since the Street Coupe is a product, and a recreational one at that, a morning news program would be the best bet, because morning TV shows are the place for soft news. Regional information is served hot—like coffee—in the morning. But even business news shows, like those found on CNBC, MSNBC, CNN, or Bloomberg, will show off a soft business story in the morning.

We'll start with the local broadcast media first. The local news shows have great viewership numbers, and they're willing to try out products like the Street Coupe. Plus, their video feeds—the raw footage they keep on hand and the ones you put onto your VCR—often find their way onto CNN, a process you can always help along later by sending a videocassette to CNN after your local segment airs. (Yes, you can do that, Virginia.)

To seize your first broadcast opportunity, pick up the phone or skate over to the local news station, show off your Street Coupe, and cut your first deal. The idea is basic: Package a nice story, letting your favorite anchor try out the skateboard while you explain how the mechanics create the dreamy ride and also where the viewers can get one. It's very important to provide everything the station wants to make the story a go. Whatever the station needs—be it volunteer kids to ride the skateboards, information on recommended safety equipment, a historical timeline of the actual skateboard—let the producer know she'll have it tomorrow morning, or later today if need be!

The other key to the presentation is to let the people involved know that your time is precious, and if they don't bite, the next station on the remote will. Good salespeople create demand, and you've got to sell the Coupe to the media. Don't fall into the trap of believing that it's such a great story that the local media will inevitably bite. Show them why it's surefire newsworthy.

The good news is that the producers of the local show bite, and the very next morning, one of the city's trusted newsmen is carving concrete with your invention. Thousands, or perhaps millions, of people are viewing your footage, thinking their husbands, wives, or kids would love to ride on a Coupe.

Within two days, you've turned your bright idea into a local hero. In the course of forty-eight hours, you've introduced your product to more than 7 million people and done it in an editorial context that builds trust and offers a third-party endorsement, something an advertisement just could never do (see sidebar, "Why Any Press Is Good Press: Not!").

A little tip: Before you leave for the studio to observe the taping of your news segment, pack a VHS tape or two with you. Make nice with the producer, and you may be able to get some immediate copies of the coverage that will be of better quality than the twice-recorded-over tape that you stick into your VCR. Like yesterday's clips, today's tape has a purpose in the near future, too.

Take It to the Top

NOW THAT THE STORY has aired on TV and put on some local muscle, it's time to take it to the nationals. San Francisco is about 3,000 miles from the media capital of the world, where all syndication and nationwide broadcasting happens—New York, but by making the right decisions, you can get there fast, and the plane can stay behind.

As with the local media, national broadcast and print media don't usually compete with each other, either. Therefore, if you play your cards intelligently, you can use one to get the other, maximize your coverage, and sell more Street Coupes. To move the print coverage past the borders of the Bay Area and into New York and every other metro area in the country, you need to seek out the syndicated wire services.

A placement in the Associated Press wire, for example, will

officially make you an expert, as far as the media's concerned. Some outlets, such as Bloomberg, Reuters, and the Associated Press, cover news around the world and distribute their stories to thousands of papers across the globe. A good syndicated story can wind up in seventy or eighty papers around the world, including *USA Today*, the *New York Times*, the *Guardian* (U.K.), *Stern*, the *Financial Times*, Japan's *Nikkei* newspaper, and the *Wall Street Journal*. This is why we counsel you to pay attention to "small" newspapers like the *Dallas Morning News*, which has great reporters (notably in the business section). Thus, its stories are picked up by many newspapers the world over, which vastly extends the reach of the press coverage for you.

Let's take the Associated Press as an example of syndicated coverage. Although it's based in New York, the Associated Press has writers stationed all over the map. Therefore, finding the one assigned to your neighborhood (and your beat) is essential. If the yellow pages don't work, try the syndicate's website for listings of the regional office closest to you. Line up your best pitch, fork over a copy of the *Examiner* article (this is why you kept extra copies, remember?), and submit a VHS tape. You could even send over someone on a skateboard. Let the AP reporter know he's the first one to give the Street Coupe a "go" outside of the Bay Area. He'll be pleased.

Wire service coverage is really not that much different from print coverage generally, except that you never know exactly when and where it will run. You can pitch, and the reporter can write the best story ever, but if none of the service's subscribers picks up the darned thing, you're *meat*. A nice AP or Reuters reporter will inform you of the story's progress, or you can just get onto their websites and follow the bouncing dateline.

Anyway, in this case, that local AP reporter sounded intrigued. He tells you he'll call you back—maybe not today, but in a few days. Keep on him, and your Street Coupe will soon be all over the afternoon wire for every local, national, and foreign

Why Any Press Is Good Press: Not!

When the press reported that Woody Allen was dating his girlfriend's daughter, the diameter of his already miniscule social circle got even smaller. For Woody, it was press he could have done without.

"Any press," as they say, doesn't always equal "good press." The rule we are shooting down doesn't apply only to celebrity family get-togethers, either. It applies to you, your company, your product, or your big idea. Bad press goes beyond the "oh my, look at what they said about me" form of dirt-dishing. Indeed there is, in the media world, a worse fate than a daily reporting on your arrest some years back, or the accounting scandal, girlfriend on the side, or bad toupee. That happens when an intrepid reporter makes news about your business and somehow misses the entire point of what you are doing.

That, friends, is a pure example of bad, meaningless press. Like sex without love, we surmise.

In 2000, the Wall Street Journal *ran a cover story on LowerMy Bills.com, a website and firm that compares your monthly bills—electric to credit cards to mobile phone charges—and pairs you up with a company willing to give you the same service but cheaper. There was*

paper to pick up and run with. Often, the story runs with graphics "supplied" by the AP (in other words, *you*).

When good stories run over the wire, the broadcast media jump on it, and you may come in one morning to find you have a message from the morning news producers in New York, Boston, or Chicago, asking for an opportunity to take the Street Coupe for a test run *live* tomorrow. Now, these shows may have millions of viewers, and they may be well-rated shows, but ... ask yourself if this is what you really want. These shows have their audiences, but they aren't national shows, per se, and there are programs with more viewers who can make your skateboards bigger. Even if you're not nationally known yet, you should be thinking this way *a coveted Journal placement with almost a full page of text, accessorized by artwork and glowing commentary. Many PR pros thought that this piece of press was, in fact, pretty terrific.*

We were smart enough to know better. It's not that the Journal gave LowerMyBills the editorial boot or panned it amongst competitors. Hardly the case: While the Journal was complimentary about the idea of a way to lower bills, the company was discussed as part of an energy conservation trend piece, which was not the firm's mission at all. In fact, the article confused the message LMB was trying to send the public about what the site and its founders were actually up to.

As expected, the article didn't end up making a dent in site traffic—very little business came of it. But the real problem wasn't the lack of response. It was more that LMB's big chance in the Journal was lost on poor messaging and sloppy definition—well, let's just say it got rushed out.

Words in a paper or on a monitor do not necessarily equal good press. If you're trying to be perceived as credible, a story about your rap sheet isn't adding to the cause, nor is a newspaper article that completely misses what you're about. No. "Just any" press is not good press. In fact, it can do you more harm than good.

in order to ramp up the level of your press coverage at this point.

Let's go for the gusto and aim for the *Today* show. America loves Matt and Katie, and you can bet having either one of them zipping around on your Coupe is guaranteed to sell thousands, if not tens of thousands, of them. Also, the Street Coupe is just the type of feel-good, innovative toys they cover. So before you get back to the Boston producer, make the pitch to someone at NBC—by e-mail, fax, and phone—and see what happens. You've come this far, and a fear of rejection is the only thing slowing you down now.

Taking your product, service, or idea from the local press to the national media in a matter of days isn't as farfetched as it sounds, and we're not suggesting the national shows simply for ego gratification. Shows like *Good Morning America* and *Today* have so many viewers that they in turn influence not only the water cooler crowd, but also pop culture in general. They affect the press, and, in a way, they make the rules, or at least the trends. After all, it's the morning—when everyone is sleepy and the subconscious rules!

The Exclusive Story

ANYWAY, BACK TO OUR SCENARIO. Someone at the *Today* show thinks that a story on the Coupe might be fun. They are indeed considering doing a piece on your skateboard, but only under certain conditions. Enter the term "exclusive." Exclusives are part of the game, and if you go about them properly you'll get the coverage you're looking for. Just as it implies, an exclusive is an agreement between you and the media that means one outlet gets the story first. This is analogous to an exclusive in the print media world (see Chapter 3 for a more detailed explanation).

There are also different types of exclusives—for print, broadcast, local radio, newsletters, corporate house organs, and so on. In your case, you couldn't offer the *Today* show a complete exclusive because your story already ran in print. You can submit to the broadcast exclusive, as the show's requesting, because luckily you and the Coupe haven't landed on TV. Not yet. What about the local TV program? It's not that it doesn't "count," per se, but to be honest, the people at *Today* aren't going to care, and if they did care, they might be impressed with your performance (don't volunteer it).

But what are the benefits? The *Today* show producers said they'd like to run it three days from now, even though the voice-mail message from the Boston network said they wanted it for tomorrow. Also, even if *Today* or any other TV program secures a time slot for you, the unpredictable news of the day can throw the reporting schedule to the wind, leaving you high and dry. But you know that the prospect of national coverage makes the risk of waiting worthwhile, so you call back the Boston producer to tell him you can't do the piece tomorrow because of the exclusive. However, you console him, you *can* do it later in the week.

The Boston producer will appreciate your honesty, and because he knows that you're a straight shooter, he says he might be interested in having you on the show later, simply because you have assured him this will be an easy segment to produce. Also, mention to the producer that he can create a quick news item about your skateboard—something that will fit into any news hour on any given news day, since it isn't attached to a particular date. That's called an evergreen story.

There's Enough for Everyone

HERE'S AN OFFBEAT EXAMPLE of how to keep all those producers happy. One of our associates had two small children in the family and a third on the way. He and his wife wondered how they were going to make ends meet, send their kids to the best schools, and still lead an enjoyable life. A marketing journalist by trade, Jason put his beat to work and decided to auction off his to-be-born son's name for corporate sponsorship. Jason asked us to help him publicize the endeavor.

Despite the craziness of the idea—not to mention the huge ethical questions—this was indeed a story. For a minimum bid of $500,000 dollars, any company could bid on eBay, the online auction service, for the right to name Jason's to-be-born son after its name or product. Pringles Black? Why not?

Since the auction was being held on eBay, a smart Web culture journalist at a national paper was the best bet to cover the story. We called one of the best journalists we know writing about the Web—Janet Kornblum of *USA Today*. At the time, her column "eLife" was documenting what people were really doing online and in technology; thousands of people read it religiously. The morning the story appeared in Janet's column, the phones started

Why Letters to the Editor Are PR

Dear Reader:
You have to remember all that democracy truly guarantees us:
death, taxes, and, according to Mark Twain, a letter to the editor.
The last is one of the most effective ways to get coverage in your
favorite magazine. (We don't suggest death or taxes.) If you're like
most people, whether you flip through Vogue *or* Computer User, *you*
set up camp for a few minutes on the "Letters to the Editor" sec-
tion to read what people are griping about, snicker at the journal-
ists' boo-boos (this is where a magazine usually runs its correc-
tions), and peek into what else readers are thinking.

There's another side to the letters section. Besides being a great
place to rant, it's also a good spot to shift opinions-at-large and plug
your business to boot. It's PR through and through.

Pick up any publication, let's say BusinessWeek, *and take a long,*
hard look at the letters. In one particular and randomly selected issue,
neatly tucked onto page 19, Richard J. Martin, executive vice presi-
dent of AT&T, takes up a full page (small print, of course!) to grind an
extremely angry ax and truly straighten out, he says, the "blatant dis-
tortions" served up in an article the week before. Now, there are two
sides to every story, and Mr. Martin decided that his side should be
long, packed with juicy sound bites, and free of editorial banter.

Martin gets away with sentences such as, "AT&T Broadband's

ringing. Jason spoke first to the AP, because no other print outlet
would be able to spread the story as quickly. Within a few hours,
it was on the AP wire for every newspaper, radio program, and TV
show to see.

From there, we gave the morning news exclusive to Katie
Couric at the *Today* show for the next morning, but that limited
him to keeping quiet for a difficult fifteen hours. Since an exclusive had been struck with the show, we turned down CNN, CNBC,

combined telephony, high-speed data and digital-video growth leads the industry," and the hearty "After AT&T Broadband spins off and merges with Comcast, AT&T will have one of the strongest balance sheets in the industry." Amen.

We're pretty sure that after BusinessWeek printed those sentences, Martin and his pals were high-fiving each other and sparking up Churchills in the conference room.

Albeit a pretty obvious example, there are hundreds of more subtle plugs in the letters section. You don't have to be a big muckety-muck setting the record straight or calling a journalist on a blunder. You can write in support of an article you've read and work your message, subdued or otherwise, into your point.

The specific purpose of the letters section is to give readers the opportunity to chime in on what's going on in the publication and society at large, so use it to your advantage and make yourself and what you're up to relevant at every opportunity. Also, reporters, dare we say, read the letters section and often snatch up great story ideas and sources this way. As Samuel Clemens once said, you have to use this gift in order to learn its value.

Yours truly,
Richard Laermer

BBC, Fox News, and many others that day, but the producers understood why and were willing to wait, as long as we handed them something unique and different for their segments.

Although Jason was the only spokesperson for the family in all the news segments, each network was able to play a different angle of the story. For instance, CNN had his older daughter of four on the air to hear her thoughts (children make for good TV!), Fox was able to pay a visit to the household, and CNBC received the first nighttime news slot interview. What was left for BBC? Why, the international angle, of course: What this would mean to babies worldwide! The point is that it's important to offer variety to different producers, letting them know you're working to give them something unique and worthy for airtime.

In addition, a Westchester correspondent for the AP received all the story developments before the rest of the print media, and we gave him the opportunity to continue reporting the story on a national level, with a new angle each week. For the next month, it was open season on the baby-naming story. Ethical debates sparked in the media, political cartoonists made light of the baby-naming phenomenon, and every pundit on earth had a swing. The story continued for a year—even though no bid for the baby's name was ever offered.

The bottom line is that once you've got the media on the hook, and someone bites, don't sit back and enjoy the attention. Make it work for you—and now. Think big; choose the smartest path to maximum exposure; and supply every producer, journalist, fact checker, and editor along the way with as much information as possible.

When you've done it right, the momentum you've created will inevitably propel you in the media for months or even years. Journalists will be intimately familiar with your story, and when similar products, events, mishaps, ideas, or opinions—yours or your company's—occur, *and you let them know,* you'll get a call back right away. It sounds daunting, but it will become much easier the second or third time. Once you've got your foot in the national media's door, you're on your way to big-time buzz.

CHAPTER 9

That Internet Chapter

NEW MEDIA. YOU HEAR IT all the time, everywhere you go. But what the heck is it? New media is nothing more than shorthand for the Internet. The Internet has become the powerhouse of the media industry, because when it comes to news, the Web offers so many more options and capabilities than the traditional print and broadcast media.

Traditional papers go to print in the wee hours. Big machines churn out millions of sheets of printed paper, assemble them, pack them up and do it all again the next night. It's a once-a-day process, and it doesn't happen any more often than that. The story's so much more exciting for the Web. It never goes to print, it's never definite, and it never closes. Or as news guys say: never frozen.

You can harness those torrents of energy and use them to generate electrifying buzz. For the past ten years we've surfed from New York to Tahiti, found some of the most useful tricks on the Web, and figured out how to convert fiber, switches, and keyboards into a turbo-charged publicity tool. This isn't a do-it-yourself guide to building a website—there are already plenty of books out there on that subject. Instead, we want this to serve as a useful, capricious, and fun primer on generating "da buzz" online and to give you the inside scoop on the current environment for media relations on the Web.

And now, on to the rules of the Web game.

You Must Be This Tall to Ride the Web

INFORMATION IS POWER. That's no mere cliché. In just about any industry, the most powerful people have the information first. The Internet's got the corner office now. For a lifetime, the *New York Times, USA Today* and their ilk were the publications to break big news. But in just a few years, the Web has forced us to change what we expect from even these gray ladies. The *Times* and *USA Today* are no longer the places to read it first; the Internet is. Sites like MSNBC.com, CNN.com, News.com, and others turned heads by reporting news moments after it happened.

Web news is as limber as it is fast. Hell-bent on speed and beating the big papers to the punch, Web news sites initially lacked the literary wordsmithing, multi-dimensional reporting, insight, and authoritative disposition of traditional papers. Since they trailed in institutional posturing, they made up for it (and still do) in personality. But Web media has outgrown most of its earlier teen tendencies and has gone mainstream. There isn't a newspaper worth reading now that doesn't have an online component to break news in some form or another. Even TV news programs have gone online to amplify past their time slots and cash in on the influence of the Web.

That said, it's still true that a different set of standards governs what's said and who says it on the Web. Online, everyone's a columnist or a publisher. Digital articles are filled with commentary, opinion, inside jokes, jabs, and jibes. Like everyone else in the "new media revolution," editors and reporters often pooh-pooh the rules of the traditional media, making anything game. The Web is a hot rumor mill, fanning sensational flames of gossip and whispering at water coolers all over.

Matt Drudge was once an unknown quantity on the beltway of American political news. As master of The Drudge Report, a mudslinging website among the button-down correspondents on The Hill, Drudge wasn't considered worth talking to. Despite the initial naysaying, the Web gave Drudge freedom—the freedom to influence everyone.

Not connected to an editorial board or to the ethos of the *Washington Post,* Drudge was free to fraternize with insiders most reporters wouldn't speak with and to make them sources. Drudge leveraged his murky Rolodex and digital autonomy to report news as rumors before it hit the front pages as facts. He built a powerful reputation and a super loyal readership. Now Matt Drudge is a real media player—hobnobbing with the insiders and playing a role in everyone's media strategy. A titillating site made him one of a handful of media personalities that actually matter in a fickle town.

Whether or not you agree with Drudge's philosophy on the news, he and online journalists like him have expanded the boundaries of what is considered newsworthy, bringing new levels of humor, irony, and personal observation to the news. And in terms of PR and buzz, the Web's flexible boundaries offer plenty of opportunities to pitch more information personally.

Good PR people aren't intimidated by the lack of rules on the Web. Instead, they turn it into an advantage. For example, since most Web editors are personas as well as journalists, they're usually willing to write about themselves as much as they are the news. Therefore, by flipping through their archived articles, you can get a very clear sense of what Web reporters like or dislike. Some (ahem, most) of them have their own websites, too, which should give you some further biographical background.

Once you know what's in their "yea" columns, pitch your product or service to them as people, not as journalists (flattery doesn't hurt at this juncture, either). As you would do for a traditional print journalist, hook them by sending a sample of your product. If all goes according to plan, you'll get a glowing review of not just the product, service, or whatever it is you're hawking, you'll also get a great story that explains how *they* used it: how it made their commute easier, how it got their floors shinier, or how it saved them from bankruptcy.

And it practically goes without saying that your product review will be published light years faster than it would be in print. Thanks to some simple circuitry, a journalist armed with a laptop and wireless modem can attend a press conference, write the story on the fly, e-mail it to her editor, and have it posted online before she even gets back to the office. Printing presses cannot compete with that. Therefore, many print newspapers depend on timely updates to their websites to narrow the speed gap between themselves and strictly online publications.

Use this to your advantage. If your news isn't big enough in the eyes of the top daily papers, go to the Web and use that as your jumping-off spot. Set your sights high here, too. Plenty of national-al weekly magazines that you've come to know and trust have online components that act as daily news centers. Forbes.com, for instance, files new stories twice a day. While traditional print reporters have a story due once every week or two, our pals on the digital side are scrambling for news all day, every day, making it much easier for you to get noticed. For the reporter, it's a found story. For you ... well, among other things, you can finally say at parties: "as I said in *Forbes* ..." in gleeful earnest.

Let's Talk about E-Mail, Baby

INCREASINGLY, E-MAIL IS the medium of choice in business communications, and that extends to media relations, too. Our research over the past two years, involving more than 400 people in public and private organizations, reveals that over 47 percent send and receive more than forty messages per day. Real e-mail addicts like us send and receive more than 500 messages per day, thanks to newfangled wireless devices.

E-mail has not replaced voice-mail yet, but it has made a dent. Many people get less voice mail now that they're heavy e-mail users. E-mail gives you the ability to send more details and better support, such as attachments. It also allows you to erase, revise, resend, reply, and rethink. For that reason, e-mail is a more thoughtful medium than voice. These days you're just as likely to hear someone say "E-mail me" as you are to hear him say "Call me."

These developments can have a big impact on the success of your media relations efforts. For example, most journalists won't bother listening to a story pitch that you leave on their voice mail. They can, on the other hand, save an interesting notion that pops into their inbox and send you a quick question back. If you're lucky, they'll cut and paste your response right into their story. This is one of the quickest, simplest, and most painless ways of getting press coverage online.

Therefore, if you're still an e-mail technophobe, take a deep breath and just get over it. To compete for press coverage, you need to be online, as well as e-mail accessible. To do that, all you need is a computer (okay, that might cost a bit, but you'll see a return in about forty-five minutes) and an Internet service provider, or ISP, such as MSN, Earthlink, Time Warner Cable, or, heaven forbid, AOL (very expensive, vintage, and not respected by many professionals on the receiving end). By signing up with any ISP, you automatically get your own address to send and receive your way to stardom. Yes, this is basic stuff, but as with many simple truths, it bears repeating.

By the way, although we're strong advocates of e-mail, we're not fans of instant messaging because currently you can't keep a record of most instant messages—although that will change soon. But the real problem is that you can babble on way too much with instant messaging (IM has no recourse and zero consequences) and can say *stupid* stuff and waste *loads* of time. Conversely, e-mail is a nice way to edit what you write, and you quickly see that there is a record of everything you say when you talk way too much.

For e-mails with the most impact, don't cut corners when you write, any more than you would with a real letter. Don't use phonetic spellings, abbreviations, all capital letters, and so forth to save a second or two. If you want to be taken seriously, do not let sloppiness creep into your correspondence. You demonstrate your intelligence by how well you convey your thoughts in writing, and journalists have a keen eye for finding mistakes.

Mind Your Electronic Manners ("E-tiquette")

Are your e-mail messages news or nuisance? Now that so many people are struggling to manage a daily stream of e-mails, you need to be sensitive to anything that could inconvenience them or cause them extra work. Here are some tips from PR people about etiquette. Please clip them to your fridge and study over your morning latte. And don't forget to use them!

1 **Keep your message short.** You don't know whether someone is picking this up on her Blackberry or other handheld, or her desktop.

2 **Do not cry wolf.** "Highest" priority should really mean what it says.

3 **Make e-mail messages easy for the recipient to file.** Write a short message on each topic rather than one long message on several. And your subject line should be explicit. (For your own e-mail filing, take advantage of your e-mail features,

such as sorting by date, name, filing, and so on.)

4 **Read over your e-mail before you send it, even when you're in a hurry!** Try to imagine you're the person reading it. And treat e-mails just as you would any other business letter—with great care. For good perspective, get a friend or business colleague to read over important e-mails before you hit Send.

5 **Make it clear to business associates and journalists whether you prefer voice mail or e-mail,** and find out what other people's media preferences are. Not everyone loves e-mail.

6 **In the body of the message, mention any attachments** and tell the recipients exactly what they contain.

7 **Read Strunk & White's** *The Elements of Style* before you write another e-mail. Do what it says. Then share it with your e-mail-ees.

8 **Use online discussion groups for virtual team working sessions,** instead of over-relying on e-mail. And call a face-to-face meeting when the "Copy All" feature is being overused in your group. And don't get us going on BCC, or blind-copy habits. That's rude and duplicitous.

9 **Your name should appear in the sender section of the e-mails you send.** No cute names, please. Because spam e-mail is becoming such a problem, many e-mail users are increasingly deleting the message before reading it if they can't identify the sender immediately.

10 **Never send e-mail when you're angry.** And we do mean *never.* Consider first sending it to yourself before hitting the ultimate "No Exit" button (Send).

11 **Assume that whatever you write in an e-mail could be printed** on the front page of the *New York Times*. E-mail, friends, isn't private.

12 **Avoid huge attachments.** Graphic files can be too large for many people to open. It's a breach of new Internet etiquette to assume that the whole world has the same access to bandwidth that you do. Instead, send a link to a website where you've got the graphics loaded. If you have to send a large attachment, warn the person to whom you're sending it. Spank people who send you large attachments without warning.

13 **Stop checking your e-mail** when your spouse wants to make love, your kid wants to talk to you, or your best friend calls and wants to chat. **And take a whole day off from e-mail now and then.**

14 **Do not check your e-mail when you're in a face-to-face meeting**, even if this is an accepted practice in your company. We guarantee that your seeming preoccupation will annoy someone, and you could miss hearing some important information. Consider what you'd want people to do when you're making a presentation or talking.

15 **Don't give out another person's e-mail address without permission.** And be careful when sending broadcast e-mails—if you don't suppress the list it's like broadcasting your contact list.

16 **Set a goal to keep the number of messages in your inbox below twenty-five.** This will bring you great stress relief. And your administrator ("tech person") will worship you.

17 **If you're going to harass someone, e-mail is not the place to do it.** This seems self-evident, but some people are dumb enough to do this. The judge and jury will waste no time convicting you after reading through your clueless e-mails. And if you employ people, make sure they're not doing it, either. You could be liable for their behavior.

18 **Write a handwritten note from time to time** instead of sending e-mail. In a world of effortless electronic correspondence, taking the time and care to send a handwritten letter says a great deal about you.

19 **Be careful when you're addressing e-mails from your address book.** It's really easy to click on the wrong "Bob."

20 **Don't assume people have definitely received your e-mail.** Servers go down, machines crash, and e-mails are misdirected. Give people the benefit of the doubt.

21 **Cut down as much as possible on the time you spend with e-mail.** If you receive fifty e-mails per day and you spend five minutes on each one, that's a little over four hours per day.

22 **When you receive e-mail from someone, pay attention to the style he uses.** Is it terse? Friendly? Imaginative? Matching a person's style when you respond can be a very effective communication approach. If the person is no-nonsense, keep your correspondence all business. If, on the other hand, the person to whom you are writing is more laid-back and mentions his vacation, don't offend him or make him feel foolish with a curt response.

A WORD OR TWO ABOUT "carbon copy" e-mails: They're like bills—no fun and far too numerous. And they are spam—meaning totally unwanted, excess *garbage*. Not only are all of us subjected to lame jokes forwarded by well-meaning but not-so-funny friends, but we're also at the mercy of marketers who are getting cleverer by the nanosecond. You know the type: They send e-mails that seem to be personalized, with innocuous subject lines that catch you off guard and prevent you from hitting the delete key immediately. From the perspective of creating buzz, this means that you should avoid using these tacks yourself, both with reporters and consumers. You won't win friends, customers, or press coverage that way. Just say no!

Once you've started exploring the possibilities of communicating with the media through e-mail, start checking into other avenues. E-mail isn't the only way to communicate online, and we're not just talking about having your own website (which you should have, by the way). Just about any industry, pastime, profession, or event has a website and some sort of public message board associated with it. The most dedicated fans of every subject go to message boards to compare notes, share info, and generate buzz.

Plus, it's a good way to find out what people really think of you. For instance, if you run a start-up sneaker company, a quick visit to **www.runnersareus.com** will produce a network of runners from around the world, comparing everything from socks to sport drinks. Posting information about your trainers will start the ball rolling and produce some quick-hit sales for you. And, of course, direct them to your site, which by now is a masterpiece. Right? Cover the waterfront, so to speak. Don't stick to one message board; try several to help increase your chances of getting a hit. That's the way to start word of mouth on the ole Web!

Get Wired

IF YOU'VE GOT SOMETHING big to say, consider using Web-based newswires. For a fee, these services will send your news release to thousands of journalists in your industry. But note that about 70 percent of the releases crossing the wire every day are bland, uninteresting announcements that no journalist would ever be interested in.

What's more, sending a release over the wire can cost anywhere from $100 to $3,000. Because we don't want you to waste your hard-earned money, we always recommend you have something *real* to announce, like landing a big tranche of investment capital or curing cancer, before you hit the send button. Provided you have the makings of a newsworthy, interesting story, a well-written release will garner you calls from giddy journalists clamoring for comment.

Two wire services top the popularity contest among journalists: Business Wire (**www.businesswire.com**) and PR Newswire (**www.prnewswire.com**). Both services let the sender target editor beats, choose the exact times of the news release, and attach photos and charts for added punch. Submitted releases are posted on the wire site and delivered via e-mail to journalists who've signed up to receive them for a particular industry. Plus, your release is maintained in an electronically archived file, which means that reporters who are writing stories related to your company or product can look up your file and view all of the releases that you've posted through the wire service.

Research and Snoop, Dawg

THE WEB WAS MADE to share information. Like the art of PR itself, communication is the backbone of the Internet. Its original intent was to connect scientists to one another and to let lab coats separated by miles and oceans share their findings (plus play a mean game of chess). Now you can learn from others' research just as effectively. Elusive searches that used to require hours in the library, sifting through microfilm (and its aquatic cousin, microfiche), now require only a few clicks in the comfort of your own home or office.

But you have to know where to start searching. As with anything else on the Web, you can do decent research for free, although more thorough examinations will cost you. However, about 99 percent of the info you need can be found on the cheap.

And don't underestimate the quality of the information you can unearth from the Web. Competitive searches, latest industry maneuverings, journalist backgrounds, and coverage earned by our clients and competitors are part of our daily digital scrutiny, and they should be a crucial part of yours, too, if you want to be effective at creating buzz. By knowing how to search and where to do it, you suddenly find yourself linked to articles, technical information, photos, and gossip on anyone or anything.

Consider a few things when starting your search. Where does your investigation stem from geographically? Is it a big news story already? Who's behind it?

Google (**www.google.com**) is the mother of all search engines and a family friend, so to speak. It snoops through more than one billion-plus Web pages to find what you're looking for, and it has a non-tech way to show you the goods. But it's better at some things than others. Google is best at finding people: where they've been, their little secrets, and their big successes. Within a few minutes, Google can piece together the biography of anyone worth searching for.

WiseNut (**www.wisenut.com**) is another site with equal or greater search relevance when compared to Google, so use them together to maximize your results. We also like **www.vivisimo.com** because of its accessible way of grouping information.

If you're looking for corporate information or the latest deal in your industry, come on over to the websites of local newspapers, which often yield decent results. Most metro papers have sites that let you search through the archives and find any story they've written over the past few years, but their search technology isn't always good or easy to use, so you might want to try different query words to uncover the right article. Older articles might cost a few dollars, but the convenience is worth it. Can you imagine going to the library to pick up one article? Time is money. Say it twice.

If your search requires something akin to sophistication, such as international news, legal documents, and other such information, go to LexisNexis (**www.nexis.com**). Unlike most services online, LexisNexis charges by the minute, so have your search carefully mapped out before handing over your Amex number. Beyond sifting though thousands of newspapers, wire services, and international news outlets, Nexis.com will also delve through hard-to-find newsletters, specialized journals, and even TV transcripts.

If you're looking for intelligence on a competitor, the right place is the company's website. Most companies have a "press room" page on their site where you can find the squeaky-clean news—such as when they started, how much money they've raised, and what deals they've cut. Nexis, Google, and the others will help you find the more scandalous gossip. Other good possibilities are the websites of analyst firms for your industry. And, of course, you can go to the rumor boards, places like Fucked Company.com, as well as the industry watchdogs often found on sites such as Yahoo!, HotJobs, and Monster.

The Web is also a great way to research the media itself—specifically, journalists whom you want to target with story pitches. Clicking through the archives of newspapers themselves will give you a great sense of what a particular journalist is interested in covering. But if you want an extra edge, there are pay services online that let you know the publication's circulation, how much ads cost, which journalist covers which beat, and even how they prefer to be pitched (i.e., via telephone, fax, snail mail, or e-mail).

Two of these standout services are Bacon's (**www.bacons newsservice.com**) and MediaMap (**www.mediamap.com**), now owned by Bacon's. Both are relatively expensive but worth the cost if you're ready to kick off a big buzz campaign. They also both have their strengths and weaknesses. For more comprehensive information, Bacon's is the best bet for the money. It gives information on all broadcast and print media outlets and all the general information you need. Its list-building capabilities are limited, and the navigation can be as clumsy as a newborn Bambi, but it delivers a complete list of media possibilities for one price. Although MediaMap does a better job, in our experience, of compiling lists, and the background on journalists is more complete, it charges individually for access to each media type, be it broadcast, international, and so on, for the same comprehensive listings that Bacon's provides.

In general, the key to research on the Web is becoming adroit at doing free or inexpensive searches, figuring out which query phrases work best, and which sites work best for you. Like any skill, Web research takes a bit of practice. Start small. Keep a pad and write down the sites that provide the best search results for you, or file them in your "favorites" folder. That will make for smoother surfing next time.

Also take special note of the actual terms you used in your search. Did you put an "and" in between "Chicago" and "messenger services" or a "+," for example? In a world of algorithmic inquiries, subtle changes will result in different findings. Most search pages, such as Google, Yahoo!, WiseNut, AltaVista, and the like have an underused button called the "advanced search." Click it and give it a try. Advanced searches let you set more parameters in your Web rummaging, such as a defined time span, selected publications, and so on. It's a good way to filter out the irrelevant and stir up only the results that matter. Finally, it's also smart to remember that time is money, so plunking down a few bucks for Lexis-Nexis or some other search service can be a good idea if it saves you hours of fruitless search time.

Give Away the Goods

ANOTHER WAY TO USE THE WEB is to distribute your positive press like a professional. In other words, give away the goods! Press begets press. It's like dating. Every industry has a handful of online Web magazines that eat up the news and build credibility for those covered. The wireless industry has FierceWireless (**www.fiercewireless.com**), the search engine industry has Search Engine Watch (**www.searchenginewatch.com**), and comic book inkers even have Comic Book Resources (**www.comicbookresources.com**). Your industry has one, too. The journalists behind these sites are usually the most knowledgeable in the field and write in-depth profiles that give the mainstream news a better sense of what the story really is.

On the flip side, just as you are researching journalists on the Web, they're hard at work researching you and your industry. Therefore, creating a website for journalists to follow up and do research of their own is one of the best ways to garner some solid press. If you don't already have a website, you can register one for $35 at Network Solutions (**www.networksolutions.com**), Domain Names (**www.domainnames.com**), or Register.com (**www.register.com**).

And if you're not a hardcore HTML junkie, don't despair. Despite what you may have been told, good websites simply don't need to be flashy, overproduced affairs. On the Web, simplicity rules, and with a beginner's guide, you can build an online press kit that gives journalists everything they need to know about you to help them fill in the blanks and connect the dots.

To start with something simple, include a backgrounder that explains the genesis of the company, what its mission is, when it was founded, and who invested in it. Here we need to add one very important note. The first page of your website should contain, in an obvious place, a quick, efficient way to contact you. The contact information should not be buried somewhere else, as it is with most corporate sites. In order to succeed in the world of exposure, you must make yourself easy to find. Nothing is more frustrating to journalists than not being able to find the person to whom they need to speak or write. Access is key to coverage, so you should make yourself easy to track down.

Your biography should be here, too, as well as those of any officers involved in the strategic direction and development of your company. Also consider a FAQ, or a page of well-written, jargon-free, frequently asked questions about your company and product. Consider the questions friends or customers ask you most often and supply the answers, giving journalists (and other nice people who might pay you something) the answers that describe you. We also recommend supplying a detailed list of services or products on this page.

You should put in a press section, too. Use this page to post all the releases that your company has published, as well as all the good press coverage you've received. Arrange it chronologically, in data order. And keep the bad press to yourself, by all means. Unless it's comical, in which case why not! Make someone happy by making her crack up.

If you happen to have the budget and gumption to punch up your site a bit and make it a bit more elegant than any starter kit can provide, spend the money and outsource the task to the professionals. They know how to avoid the extremely time-intensive and expensive pitfalls amateurs fall into, and chances are they have some sort of template on their desktop that can get you up and running quickly.

By the way, don't fret about keeping up with the updates. Today Web creators will create a simple and inexpensive template for you and show your staff how to update the website, so you don't have to pay the website designer every time you make a change. It's called neo-realism, as opposed to the phony, self-important manner in which '90s Web companies forced people to go to them for every single expensive amendment.

Once your website is live, don't stop there. Have a page where surfers can find fresh content, such as interesting columns and commentary on your industry. If there's quality in the writing (a trait very hard to find on the Web) and if it's updated regularly, you'll create a following of people who make your site part of their weekly Web expedition.

Modem Operandi: Online Gadgets and Gizmos

NOW THAT YOU'VE TRUDGED through a few basics of using the Net, it's time for the fun stuff—everything you need to know about what's available to you! Here is all that techno, whiz-bang stuff that you can leverage to begin creating more exposure for your company. A lot of these tools are time-tested, proven, and reliable. Others are so brand new that we have to sigh and wonder, but we still think they're pretty terrific. We've also included tools that you can download and informational updates that you can request via e-mail.

Zoomerang (www.zoomerang.com)
If you've ever flipped through the pages of *USA Today,* you've noticed their famous informational graphics. Photo editors love making printable charts out of surveys, and for you, they're a great way to qualify your claim, whatever it is, with the media.

Another great use for charts is to analyze the response to the buzz you've gotten already. Let's say your scooter company has really taken off in Atlanta, and your scooters are everywhere, in corporate parks and schoolyards alike. You might consider a localized survey aimed at finding out if local commuters have considered new alternatives to the traffic in the last three months. Should the response be encouraging (and that depends a great deal on how the questions are phrased), you can be certain the local news stations would love to feature the hard numbers on their evening news shows, fully equipped with workers buzzing around on your zippy scooters.

The problem is, as any college sophomore squeaking by on his statistics requirement will tell you, that actually getting a survey to work for you is one part skill, two parts miracle. Zoomerang is a nifty website that helps you ask the right questions and then send them out to the right group of people based on age, region, and other demographics. The best part is that Zoomerang will do the math for you, too, so you can make sense of it all.

Professor Russell Barclay, Ph.D., and chair of the media studies and public relations department at Connecticut's Quinnipiac University's School of Communications uses Zoomerang with his students to test their theories. For no cost, his students are able to add a question or two to a survey that's going out already. This allows them to match their demographic and tap into the social consciousness, to see if big news or trends are registering with people in the same way the media or business community thinks it is.

Individuals can get some free play in this way at Zoomerang, too, but going for the full service is recommended. Why, you ask? Because, as with anything else, you get what you pay for. When you pay for the service, you can ask more people more questions, thus creating a better-rounded survey.

Media Life Magazine (www.medialifemagazine.com)

Media Life magazine is a free, digital daily magazine that covers what's going on in the media and American culture in general. Media Life usually spots trends quickly, making it a must-read to find out where you or your big idea fits into the big picture. Use its coverage to enhance your pitch and make it more relevant to the consciousness of the nation. Ah, America.

Conferenza (www.conferenza.com)

Our clients usually come to us with bloated trade show budgets and sales teams scattered across the country, manning booths and passing out business cards. The reality though is that they're spending precious time preaching to the choir and reciting their sales pitch for competitors. Depending on your industry, valuable tradeshows that put you in front of paying customers are few and far between. To sort through the ocean of convention centers, conferences, and expos, click over to Conferenza's site and zoom in on the secret of trade shows—those with a technology bent, anyway—and industry events.

Newsletters and other articles on the site let you know which companies are sponsoring shows and which companies will attend, as well as news on their development. From this information, you can get a pretty good sense of whether it's worth attending, much less fashioning a booth for. We used Conferenza recently to check out some shows that a search engine client of ours wanted to attend, and the site basically spilled the beans that all twelve of them weren't worth the time or the fare for coach seats on the plane.

We also learned from Conferenza that most of the best conferences, meaning the ones that sell products, aren't that well known. Search the shows by industry and focus on finding the ones that best match what or to whom you're trying to sell.

Multivision (www.multivision.com)

Once the Associated Press picks up your story, you're well on your way to being a star, but not quite yet. The AP, Bloomberg News, and more obscure syndicated services, such as Block Consumer News, send their stories out to thousands of networks and outlets. If you're lucky enough to be covered by the AP or any of the others, you'd better know which newspapers or broadcasters picked up the story and where. Multivision is a news tracker that basically "Googles" TV broadcasts. It can tell you where your story ran and on which networks, when and how often.

They'll also burn the coverage onto a digital videodisc, copy it to a VHS tape, or digitize it and make it available to you on the Web.

Smart PR folks use Multivision to find out exactly where their story placed. Once you know where your story aired, you can call all the other stations in the area and serve up the opportunity to be in step with their broadcast competitors, thus never missing a great news opportunity.

SourceaSaurus (www.sourceasaurus.com)

SourceaSaurus is a clever service. It's a database of "experts" for journalists to search through when they quickly need a comment from an expert qualified to address some aspect of their story. The benefit for you is that you get to make yourself an expert! The service is broken down into different topics, from food service to software, and you can list your name, background information that explains why you're a relevant source, and your contact information.

Try to keep your listing updated, and classify yourself under listings that have seasonal importance. For instance, design engineers might fare well by listing themselves under automotive design in the months before the annual Detroit car show.

PR Source Code (www.prsourcecode.com)

If you aren't monitoring the editorial calendars of all the magazines you should be in, you're destined for failure. Profiles and interviews in the media aren't enough for long-term press success. Feature articles found in editorial calendars compare the best businesses in the industry and lay out which businesses are the ones to watch—and you need to be there. Not being included wreaks havoc on your credibility and puts you in the publicity backseat. But finding editorial calendars isn't easy, and finding out who actually writes them is practically impossible. Publications usually leave out most of the info PR people need, making it hard to get noticed and included.

PR Source Code just released "Edit Forum," a tracking system that lists all the editorial calendars out there by industry and date and also gives you the actual information you need. Beyond the date the article is slated to run and its name, PR Source Code lets you know who's writing it, their contact data, a summary of the article, and the date the article is due to be submitted, rather than the date that the magazine is on sale. Knowing when an article is printing and who's responsible gives you an edge over competitors. For once, *those jokers* can be the ones wondering why they didn't get into an article, while you're having a copy of your glorious press coverage framed for the office.

eNVOLV Solutions (www.envolv.com)

If a journalist isn't getting the information she needs on you or your business, she'll abandon the story and find another one. The media window of opportunity is narrowing, and there's more news out there than ever, so if a reporter has to work to get the basics, the story will never see the light of day.

To help you get the nitty-gritty info into the media's hands, eNVOLV Solutions created Relationship Builder, a digital press kit allowing you to display more info about you and your businesses than you can in any regular paper press kit, including video clips and print-ready photography. You don't have to be a digital wiz, either. Just drop your logos, graphics, and info into the fields that have already been created, and you're done.

Eric Gerstman of Neale May & Partners in San Francisco uses eNVOLV's digital kits in some clever ways. Before sending a client off to speak at an event, he sends out links to the kit to everyone in attendance, so that they're well prepped for the lecture in advance. He also adds the link to press releases. That way, if a journalist's interest is even mildly piqued, he has all the info in front of him before his interest cools.

For the self-starter in every PR person, eNVOLV's digital kits are a cheap alternative to paper. Traditional kits worth handing out can cost up to $70 apiece, when all is said and done. You'll spend most of your time trying *not* to hand them out! With an eNVOLV link, you can dish out press kits to your heart's content.

Trash Proof News Releases (www.trashproofnewsreleases.com)

Paul Krubin is a long-time PR guru who has pretty accurately boiled down the science of getting coverage into a mathematical equation: PA+A+H = C. To the less wacky (us), Paul's mathematics means personal adversity plus achievement and a bit of humor equals coverage. Paul says that the equation plays out on the front-page *USA Today* photo every day, so if you want coverage, you're going to have to follow suit.

At Trash Proof News Releases, Paul takes your news, and for $200 or less (depending on how much research and time he must allot) he'll write you what he calls a trash-proof news release of your own that puts his algorithm to the test. For newcomers to the process, it's worth giving TPNR a go. There's a special formula that goes into successful press releases, and having others help you out with the first few is a good way to learn the process.

MediaSurvey (www.mediasurvey.com)

Sam Whitmore knows what it takes to get into the big glossy business magazines. He used to be the editor of *PC Week,* and he was a senior writer at *Fortune,* too. To help out PR people and journalists alike, he put together MediaSurvey, a site that makes sense of publications and brings together PR folks and reporters to discuss the issue at hand.

First of all, by hanging out on the site, users get access to news profiles that tell you exactly what portion of magazines are dedicated to case-study material, product reviews, profiles, and so on. If you've been pitching a profile to *Red Herring* for four months without a return call, for example, Sam's site can help you out by letting you know that most of the magazine's coverage comes from case-study material, and that this is the better route to take if you want the ink.

Besides clearly laying out the anatomy of every magazine worth reading, Sam connects influential writers with eager PR people over the phone. On a regular basis, journalists from *Forbes, Fortune, BusinessWeek,* and others join Sam and registered PR people for a conversation about issues on media relations and other, more general topics. Reporters let you know where they stand on different issues, and flacks can ask questions, pitch related stories, and help shape their coverage. (By the way, we can use the word flack [or flak—either way]. We live for this business—we're allowed!)

News Talkers (www.mdsconnect.com)

One of our favorite new services on the Web, MDS Connect's News Talkers gives a video and a venue to PR personas with something to say quickly. Like video news releases, or VNRs, News Talkers give you video capabilities to beam your footage and thoughts to the broadcast (TV and radio) media. But instead of the canned corporate statement that VNRs typically feature, News Talkers employs a seasoned interviewer to ask you real questions about your announcement, giving other producers a better sense of what the real news is behind the spin.

News Talkers is also unlike VNRs in that it isn't distributed via satellite, but through the Internet, so that the nonbroadcast media get an opportunity to take a peek. There are plenty of good uses for News Talkers—reacting to current events seems to be one of the best. Let's say you sell security equipment, and there's a rash of break-ins in the neighborhood one evening. In an hour or less, you can have a video out to the media instructing residents on what they can do to protect themselves and what products are available to them. It makes good sense and good TV!

Media Bistro (www.mediabistro.com)

Going onto Media Bistro as a PR person is kind of like spying on the media itself! This site, for unemployed writers looking for their next gig, is sort of a Monster.com for scribes—that is, journalists. But besides all the job-finding help, Media Bistro serves up daily content about the news within the news biz—for example, which magazines are launching a news section, the maneuverings of highly read journalists, which networks are booming and which ones are flopping, and all sorts of industry rumors. Keeping up with the articles on Media Bistro means you're keeping up with the ever expanding and contracting media culture that is so vital to spreading the word about your products.

Jack Myers's Report (www.myers.com)

Thankfully, Jack is a total broadcast guy—the type who arranges *all* of his furniture at home to allow him to see the boob tube from any seat in the house. As a total media business hound, Jack appears on Tech TV to dish dirt and useful information on the biz, and the advertising industry trusted him to lead the delegation to the White House Conference on Children's Television, so you can rest assured he knows what he's talking about.

His self-titled report is a must-read for those of us after small-screen fame. Day after day Myers churns out news—not about Katie Couric's quadrillion-dollar contract and new coiffure, but about how cable operators are becoming more dependent on programmer support and what role consumer technology will play in broadcast programming. For the PR enthusiast, Myers's report gives some pointers into what networks and programs are thinking and where their focus is headed. It's useful information, and reading it will allow you to at least carry on a convincing conversation with producers when the opportunity arises.

Shadow TV (www.shadowtv.com)

If your PR starts rocking and rolling and you find TV coverage for your product popping up in unlikely places, if your competitor is popping up all over and you need a handle on it, or if you're tracking a syndicated news piece in which you appeared, click over to

Shadow TV and test out their "monitor TV" service, a little "kluge"—that is, not quite perfect but worth attempting.

Basically, it's like all of your traditional monitoring services, but it differs in two major ways. With most monitoring services, if you aren't a huge client, you have to call in and tell them what you're trying to find. Then a humanoid goes through the reels, finds it and sends you the tapes in the mail. The next time you want something, you call and repeat the process.

With Shadow TV, your query or queries are recorded digitally, and the service sniffs out what you're looking for, around the clock. The other big difference is that ShadowTV won't send you a clunky VHS tape. Instead, it streams the coverage digitally right to your desktop. This way you can actually share the stream and use it with your digital propaganda campaign to take over the world.

I-PR (www.http://www.adventive.com/lists/ipr/summary.html)
I-PR is one of the best interactive PR boards still buzzing away. Thousands of PR people go online and put their heads together to imagine how to spread the buzz on the Web. They talk about everything, from how to pitch on the Net to which Web columns work best for building coverage and infamy, online and offline.

AS YOU CAN SEE, the Web is endless, and so are its possibilities. Everyone will tell you that it's all been done before, but pay no attention. Even the most talented surfers find new ways to use the Web every day, and the faster you make the digital realm part of your process, the faster your coverage will spread. Your market will expand past its borders, and your profile will rise above the competition's. The Web can be the catalyst for your success if used to its capacity. Use it well and use it carefully, just as you would any powerful tool.

Why PR Doesn't Happen Overnight

DESPITE THE FACT that news happens pretty much while you sleep, PR is surely not an overnight process (to say the least). In PR, as with so many facets of life, patience is a virtue.

We hear about "instant gratification" every day. Everything from digitally recording boob tubes to Lipton's Cold Brew teabags is engineered to give us exactly what we want when the whim overtakes us. Unfortunately, to really savor both little and big luxuries, you have to earn them. Waiting for the tea to brew and cool is a chore that takes time, but when it's ready to be served, it's a brew that's far better than that from a scientific teabag ever could be.

The same goes for getting media coverage. Never expect a catchy pitch letter to reap mounds of press just because *you* like it.

Those pieces of correspondence that you so adore, the phrases you think are so amazing—the real news is that only you may think so.

There's simply no *just add water* solution. Great PR takes time, patience, and a lot of talent, time, and effort. Anyone can land *a* story with enough phone calls, but remember, that's not the goal. What you're ultimately trying to achieve is to communicate through the media how your products or services promote exciting cultural developments, shifts, or trends.

That's no small feat. We live in a society overburdened with media, one in which all of us are bombarded by information from the TV, the radio, the Web (darn those pop-up ads), and billboards. We are constantly assaulted by information. Few spaces are private anymore—think about all the advertising you see on the backs of cabs and in elevators. In this environment, making your message seem important simply isn't an overnight job.

Let's take TiVo's digital video recorders as an example of the story behind a seemingly "overnight" success. TV technologists at TiVo started spreading the buzz well before their apparatus was available. They were smart enough to know that there were some perception potholes in the minds of consumers that would need paving before any couch potato would plunk down a few hundred bucks to bring a DVR home. "I just got a DVD player, what do I need this for?" "Monthly fees on top of cable?" "Are commercials really the enemy?" And, of course, "Harrumph! Sounds complicated! Is there a manual I gotta read?"

And yet, over the course of a few seasons, TiVos "suddenly" were being heralded as the invention of the decade. There's a lot of strategy behind what looks like an overnight success, and strategizing and planning take time.

Many people misunderstand the whole point of PR. At our firm we often cluck at the naysayers, those people who think there is a quick fix and that everything can be solved with one decent piece of press.

The awesome undertaking of a successful PR campaign is

building brand and awareness on a grand scale. You're using the press to sway opinions. What's more, you're posting a detour sign on the road of the natural course that the media follows to make a tiny piece into a national phenomenon. It takes a while to make the phenomenon real, so when a first month's worth of work hasn't panned out into gobs of coverage, remember that you're a month closer to the pinnacle of success. Don't confuse that slow but steady upward climb with being down in the gorge of failure. You may still have a long way to go, but you need to feel good about how far you've come.

HERE'S HOPING THE GODS OF PR shine upon you. With a head start, the odds are certainly in your favor.

The Cool Sources for a PR Wiz

FOR THE PR PRO who really understands that you can't do it alone, here are the best tools at your disposal. These websites will help fill in the gaps in your knowledge and resources.

Art Machine   *www.artmachine.com*

Art Machine—one of the few successes in a crowded field of PR firm aids—helps larger companies manage, distribute, and track usage of brand content (basically any piece of propaganda with your logo on it)—all on the Web. The smart idea behind it all is that you, the mobile exec, or your roving sales team sprawled out across the country can dial in from anywhere and get access to any corporate sales and marketing materials, everything from sales sheets and product descriptions to PowerPoint presentations and video footage. Art Machine will also build a digital press kit for you, too, where the media can click on icons to find head shots, B-rolls, and all sorts of public information. When your press really begins to roll and you need help managing it, Art Machine is worth checking out.

Buzz Your   *www.buzzyour.com*

This is a "how to" website that you should drop by early on your road to media stardom. It's all about creating your own buzz, not by taking on the world your first day, but by building a serious groundswell of interest in your niche—something we get into a little later on in this primer, too. The focus of the site is on a collection of Cliff Notes–looking e-books (or SparkNotes, if you're smart and modern) that give indoctrination on

- ❑ What's buzz?
- ❑ How do you get it?
- ❑ Who are good buzz builders?
- ❑ What does brainstorming have to do with it?
- ❑ Is buzz really elusive, or can you jump-start it?
- ❑ What does a PR expert say about the best and the worst ways to get buzz?
- ❑ Who are some superior buzzers, and what have they done that you can do?

The site offers specific buzz suggestions for your published book, website, or magazine.

E Releases   *www.ereleases.com*

This is a general distribution website that puts your announcements in front of its more than 2,400 journalist subscribers to help you generate some serious press. With a few clicks you can customize which type of journalists (sorted geographically, by media type, beat, etc.) you want your release sent to, to make sure what you're putting out there is read by the right people.

This all costs money. Press releases up to 500 words are $299 and $50 for each additional 100 words. The company claims to be different from the competition by not charging a membership fee. That is different.

ENewsRelease   *www.enewsrelease.com*

ENewsRelease provides PR professionals with quality media database and news distribution services. It offers professional list creation, updating of media contacts, press release distribution, and more.

Internet Media Fax   *www.imediafax.com*

Internet Media Fax is a fax news release distribution service. It offers recommendations on how to improve your news release and a customized media list recommendation. The service allows you to send your news release right to editors' fax machines.

The Journalist's Toolbox   *www.journaliststoolbox.com*

The Journalist's Toolbox features more than 6,500 websites helpful to the media and anyone else doing research. Search the site, or use an alphabetical site map or pull-down menu to locate information from a variety of news and industry-related topics, both mainstream and offbeat. For example, suppose you've developed a new type of disease-resistant corn, and you need to know which farms received federal money last year, and how much. Toolbox can help you out.

O'Dwyer's   *www.odwyerpr.com*

Jack O'Dwyer is a true PR vet who talks the talk. His newsletter—a scant eight pages—offers tips and stories that, like the other newsletters, will keep you up to speed with that's going on with journalists, trends, and tactics. *O'Dwyer's* also delves into the industry news, giving readers tips on who's looking for PR and what big accounts just got scooped up.

O'Dwyer's PR Marketplace is a mere $24 a year, and it's all about jobs. Thousands of job openings are here, and people in the business do depend upon it. If you subscribe to any of the other O'Dwyer's newsletters, you get the Marketplace gratis.

O'Dwyer's 2002 PR Buyer's Guide is just $50 and is a bible of sorts. The seventy-one-page directory lists 1,500 products and services for the PR industry in fifty-six categories, including annual report design, photo distribution, media lists, and site development. Considering he's been doing it since 1987, you know he knows everyone, that Jack.

PartyLine   www.partylinepublishing.com

The yellow-papered PartyLine is the best at tracking which journalists have gone where. Lately, with all the layoffs and fallout, it's not as easy as it sounds. In the end, knowing who is where and which stories they're covering before the rest of the field gives you the pitch advantage and is well worth the $200 subscription fee. A highly recommended read.

PR Made Easy   www.prmadeeasy.com

This site is a resource for those who want to learn how to do PR themselves. Geared toward small businesses and entrepreneurs starting out, there are five courses available, to get you on your way. From "Demystify the Media" to "How to Write a Press Release," the courses are grounded in simplicity and fundamentals.

PR News   www.prandmarketing.com

Expensive at $497 per year, PR News is nevertheless a decent and dense resource for expert news and strategies on PR and marketing. From IR (investor relations) to interactive marketing, it has tips galore—and good writing. Find news and tips on

❑ Crisis management
❑ Interactive PR
❑ Marketing and communications (MARCOM) tips

❑   Measurement, or "How'd I do?"
❑   Media relations ideas
❑   Guest columnists
❑   Interactive marketing
❑   Market research

PR Newswire   *www.prnewswire.com*

PR Newswire offers a large array of "tools of the trade," products and services for PR agencies and their clients, as well as in-house PR professionals. In addition to news and photo distribution services, PRN offers homebrew goodies such as eWatch—an online monitoring service that tracks what is being said about an organization, its competitors, or its industry on the Internet. It is attached to your electronic news release and sends an e-mail report of coverage to you as the news release appears on leading portals and websites.

The online service, eWatch Complimentary Monitoring, automatically delivers timely PR Newswire, Dow Jones, and Reuters stories that mention your organization. The Online MEDIAtlas allows you to reach more than 433,000 journalists at 127,000 media outlets worldwide through its database.

Tbutton Interactive News Release adds interactivity in the form of a link embedded in the release. The link connects online readers of the release to a brief survey, where they can provide feedback. The survey feedback helps gauge reaction to the news and gives general information about who is reading the releases on the Web. Finally, Network News Recap is a daily summary of stories covered by major network TV news broadcasts. The summary is sent to you daily via e-mail, in a digest format that shows the topic, journalist, and summary and duration of the interview.

PR Week   *www.prweekus.com*

Based in New York, with full-time correspondents in Washington, D.C.; San Francisco; and Chicago, this is a weekly magazine offering nationwide coverage of the public relations business—

along with job opportunities for PR professionals across the United States. There's news about agencies and which clients they've just scored, which campaigns have won and which ones have failed, problems affecting the PR industry, and commentary from PR pros on the industry at large.

PRanywhere
www.pranywhere.com

Part of the LexisNexis media kingdom, PRanywhere.com is a Web-based contact management system that not only lets you search for the right editor to pitch your story to but also gives you detailed info on the editors: whether they prefer e-mail pitches versus phone calls, what times are best to pitch them, and what they look for in a relationship. So that you don't make a fool of yourself, the site helps you avoid pitching to the same person twice. PRanywhere also lets you annotate the database with notes for each conversation.

Of course, PRanywhere isn't the only service on the Web like this, but it's one of the fastest and easiest-to-use databases available, and when you're trying to put a media list together or do research, speed and simplicity are job one.

Press Access
www.pressaccess.com

P/A, which is now part of LexisNexis, doles out helpful nuggets of knowledge for anyone who needs research material on the double. What's more, they've integrated their research and media pieces to create a service that lets you search for an individual journalist's articles on a particular topic, articles about selected companies, and all the research material they can muster to support your search. There's also *The Scoop,* a webzine that gives an insider's look at new magazine sections; alerts about those that have shut down; and cool, original articles and columns about everything from lifestyle news to media movers and shakers.

You can use the search engine for free, but if you want to view an article, that'll cost a few bucks. To get on and use the service, you have to work out an annual contract with LexisNexis, based on your assumed usage time (call them at 617-542-6670, ext. 402). It can get expensive, so make sure you log off whenever you're through.

Public Relations Tactics

PR Tactics is the monthly print newspaper (sorry, no Web version) of the Public Relations Society of America. PRSA is the world's largest organization for public relations professionals. Basically, *PR Tactics* provides those in the industry practical information to improve job performance and to stay competitive.

The paper publishes news, trends, and how-to information about the practice of public relations and is written by experienced PR professionals. It costs $40 per year. PRSA also publishes *The Public Relations Strategist,* a quarterly publication that focuses on strategic issues in the practice of public relations.

Publicity Hound   *www.publicityhound.com*

The Publicity Hound is a bimonthly, eight-page subscription newsletter featuring tips, tricks, and tools for free publicity. The newsletter costs $49.95 a year, which in this day and age is a bargain. Joan Stewart, a former newspaper editor and reporter, shares the secrets of how to do your own inexpensive self-promotion. Features include:

❑ How you can promote on a shoestring budget
❑ Advice from editors, reporters, authors, news directors, and radio show hosts on how to get into their publications or onto their shows
❑ Cool websites that will help you self-promote now
❑ Seasonal story ideas
❑ Secrets from some of the nation's foremost experts on how to create publicity
❑ Personal tips from Joan on how to work with the media (including the media's pet peeves)

□   Success stories about how others attracted great publicity
□   Freebies you can find through the mail or on the Internet

And of course, Joan's own personal spin. All in all, it's a useful site with great pointers on dealing with the media, one on one.

Ragan Communications, Inc.
www2.ragan.com/html/main.isx

Lawrence Ragan Communications, Inc. has been the leading publisher of corporate communications, public relations, and leadership development newsletters for more than twenty-five years. The weekly *Ragan Report* has been up, running, and successful since 1970. The Ragan brand now includes more than sixteen targeted newsletters in the areas of employee communication, Web PR, organizational writing and editing, sales and marketing, media relations, motivational management, and investor relations.

Relegence
www.relegence.com

Relegence puts information and coverage in your hands once it goes online or is made public. The service simultaneously (and amazingly) monitors, indexes, and filters more than 20,000 live streams—local and international newswires, websites, bulletin boards, television and cable networks—and delivers the information you request based on the search criteria you set up. Note that Relegence is a subscription service.

Vocus
www.vocus.com

Vocus.com provides a completely Web-based, automated public relations platform for the PR industry. Clients include PR agencies, corporations, associations, and government agencies.

The company's bag of tricks includes Vocus Media Management, which manages media relationships by keeping you posted on who's picking up your news, and Vocus Clippings Management, a Web gadget that collects and manages clips electronically and then groups them by key word, date, or topic. Vocus Publicity Management helps you manage events, such as speaking engagements, trade shows, and editorial calendars. PR Portfolio allows you to create a central knowledge base for proprietary company information for easily shared access.

One of the most obvious benefits of this system is "access anywhere." In other words, since the software is all on the Web, you can send releases from Kinko's or your Mom's. This is one of a few services that you can use offline without fancy-shmancy tools at your disposal.

Index

INDEX

About Bloomberg

Bloomberg L.P., founded in 1981, is a global information services, news, and media company. Headquartered in New York, the company has sales and news operation worldwide.

Bloomberg, serving customers on six continents, holds a unique position within the financial services industry by providing an unparalleled range of features in a single package known as the BLOOMBERG PROFESSIONAL® service. By addressing the demand for investment performance and efficiency through an exceptional combination of information, analytic, electronic trading, and Straight Through Processing tools, Bloomberg has built a worldwide customer base of corporations, issuers, financial intermediaries, and institutional investors.

BLOOMBERG NEWS®, founded in 1990, provides stories and columns on business, general news, politics, and sports to leading newspapers and magazines throughout the world. BLOOMBERG TELEVISION®, a 24-hour business and financial news network, is produced and distributed globally in seven different languages. BLOOMBERG RADIO℠ is an international radio network anchored by flagship station BLOOMBERG® 1130 (WBBR-AM) in New York.

In addition to the BLOOMBERG PRESS® line of books, Bloomberg publishes *BLOOMBERG MARKETS™* and *BLOOMBERG WEALTH MANAGER®*. To learn more about Bloomberg, call a sales representative at:

London	+44-20-7330-7500
New York:	+1-212-318-2000
Tokyo:	+81-3-3201-8900

About the Author

Richard Laermer, CEO of RLM Public Relations, is a recognized authority on media culture and co-host of the TLC series *Taking Care of Business.* The author of *trendSpotting* (Perigee), *Native's Guide to New York* (W. W. Norton), and *Bargain Hunting in Greater New York* (Prima), he appears regularly on Public Radio's *Marketplace* program. A favorite of almost all frequent flier programs, Laermer travels constantly and speaks at corporate PR divisions, marketing and networking organizations, colleges, and Fortune 100 companies.

Laermer has a background as a journalist whose work has appeared in more than fifty newspapers and magazines. He is contributing editor to *PR News,* and his monthly segment, "Unspun with Richard Laermer," appears on NY1 on Time Warner Cable. He writes "Ask the Expert" for NewYorkBusiness.com and provides provocative commentaries on PR and real life for the pages and airwaves of MediaBistro, *Advertising Age, Ad Week,* and several radio talk shows.

With RLM's erudite staff, Laermer concocts a newsletter, "The Full Frontal PR Report," which you can get free via **www.fullfrontalpr.com,** or by sending a note to **editor@RLMpr.com.**

In 1991, Richard Laermer founded RLM Public Relations, a PR firm serving consumer, technology, business-to-business, health-care, entertainment, publishing, financial services, and issues-oriented clients using the Full Frontal Approach.® With locations in NY, LA, Washington DC, Pittsburgh, and Tampa, RLM specializes in building local, regional, national, and global buzz with consumer, trade, and business constituents.

RLM creates comprehensive PR programs that deliver tangible and measurable results and drive clients' business goals. RLM's services include brand building, messaging, event planning and execution, competitive market and industry analysis, and creation of collateral materials—all with a strong and clear program replete with on-message media relations.

By identifying unambiguous objectives and determining how PR achieves those goals efficiently, aggressively, and effectively, RLM designs and implements PR campaigns with clear ROI. For information and a full list of clients and capabilities, go to **www.RLMpr.com.**